The Role of Information in U.S. Concepts for Strategic Competition

CHRISTOPHER PAUL, MICHAEL SCHWILLE, MICHAEL VASSEUR, ELIZABETH M. BARTELS, RYAN BAUER

Prepared for United States European Command
Approved for public release; distribution unlimited

 RAND NATIONAL DEFENSE RESEARCH INSTITUTE

T0002915

For more information on this publication, visit **www.rand.org/t/RRA1256-1**.

About RAND

The RAND Corporation is a research organization that develops solutions to public policy challenges to help make communities throughout the world safer and more secure, healthier and more prosperous. RAND is nonprofit, nonpartisan, and committed to the public interest. To learn more about RAND, visit www.rand.org.

Research Integrity

Our mission to help improve policy and decisionmaking through research and analysis is enabled through our core values of quality and objectivity and our unwavering commitment to the highest level of integrity and ethical behavior. To help ensure our research and analysis are rigorous, objective, and nonpartisan, we subject our research publications to a robust and exacting quality-assurance process; avoid both the appearance and reality of financial and other conflicts of interest through staff training, project screening, and a policy of mandatory disclosure; and pursue transparency in our research engagements through our commitment to the open publication of our research findings and recommendations, disclosure of the source of funding of published research, and policies to ensure intellectual independence. For more information, visit www.rand.org/about/principles.

RAND's publications do not necessarily reflect the opinions of its research clients and sponsors.

Published by the RAND Corporation, Santa Monica, Calif.
© 2022 RAND Corporation
RAND® is a registered trademark.

Library of Congress Cataloging-in-Publication Data is available for this publication.

ISBN: 978-1-9774-0876-1

Cover images: globe—piranka/Getty Images; chess—Anusorn/Adobe Stock; radio—Lance Cpl. Mackenzie Binion/U.S. Marine Corps.

Limited Print and Electronic Distribution Rights

This publication and trademark(s) contained herein are protected by law. This representation of RAND intellectual property is provided for noncommercial use only. Unauthorized posting of this publication online is prohibited; linking directly to its webpage on rand.org is encouraged. Permission is required from RAND to reproduce, or reuse in another form, any of its research products for commercial purposes. For information on reprint and reuse permissions, please visit www.rand.org/pubs/permissions.

About This Report

There is emerging consensus that the United States needs to reject the traditional notion that peace and war are dichotomous states. Competition today occurs in the space between these two poles. Strategic competition is a long game between those with a vested interest in preserving the international order of rules and norms dating back to the post–World War II era and revisionist powers seeking to disrupt or reshape this order. Competitors gain an advantage when they can harness all elements of national power—diplomatic, information, military, and economic—but success hinges on the effective use of the information environment, in particular.

This research aimed to refine concepts for operations in the information environment (OIE) and for leveraging the information joint function at the competition end of the conflict continuum. To that end, this report examines differing views on competition and distills them into a usable framework of challenges and solutions. A second component of this study involved a series of tabletop exercises with OIE practitioners, the results of which were provided to the sponsor to help improve command and control for OIE and to promote greater integration and coordination with joint, interagency, international, and multinational partners.

This project builds on a larger body of RAND Corporation work exploring competition-focused activities and providing guidance for U.S. government officials as they think about and organize for competition. An effective competitive posture will prepare the United States to thwart future aggression from adversaries that already threaten U.S. and allied interests. The results of this research should be of interest to U.S. Department of Defense (DoD) personnel with equities related to the information environment and those responsible for staff structures and command relationships at or in support of the geographic combatant commands.

The research reported here was completed in May 2021 and underwent security review with the sponsor and the Defense Office of Prepublication and Security Review before public release.

Human Subject Protections (HSP) protocols were used in this study in accordance with the appropriate statutes and DoD regulations governing HSP. Additionally, the views of the sources rendered anonymous by HSP are solely their own and do not represent the official policy or position of DoD or the U.S. government.

RAND National Security Research Division

This research was sponsored by U.S. European Command's (USEUCOM's) Information Directorate, J39, and conducted within the International Security and Defense Policy Center of the RAND National Security Research Division (NSRD), which operates the National

Defense Research Institute (NDRI), a federally funded research and development center sponsored by the Office of the Secretary of Defense, the Joint Staff, the Unified Combatant Commands, the Navy, the Marine Corps, the defense agencies, and the defense intelligence enterprise.

For more information on the RAND International Security and Defense Policy Center, see www.rand.org/nsrd/isdp or contact the director (contact information is provided on the webpage).

Acknowledgments

We would like to express our gratitude to several people in our sponsoring office who dedicated their time and expertise to enhancing the utility of this research. They included, at the time this research was completed, COL Ryan Keating, CDR Ryan Murphy, and Alan Bal. We also extend our thanks to CAPT Wendy Snyder, chief of public affairs at USEUCOM; COL Rob Kjelden of the USEUCOM Communications Strategy Division; and COL Will Freds from the Russia Strategic Initiative.

We are grateful to the RAND International Security and Defense Policy Center management team—at the time of our study, Christine Wormuth, Michael Spirtas, and Agnes Schaefer—who provided oversight and helpful guidance to ensure the quality and impact of this research. Other RAND colleagues provided thoughtful comments and critiques as we developed our tabletop exercises and thought through alternative command-and-control structures. We specifically thank Jonathan Welch, Alyssa Demus, Kimberly Jackson, William Courtney, Bruce McClintock, Clinton Reach, Dara Massicot, David Ochmanek, Gene Germanovich, J. D. Williams, John Gordon, Marta Kepe, Raphael Cohen, and Stephanie Pezard for their contributions to our thinking and our awareness of related research. We also owe a debt of gratitude to our reviewers, Alyssa Demus and Michael Williams, who read and provided valuable feedback on a draft of this report as part of RAND's quality assurance process. Lauren Skrabala provided invaluable advice and service when we asked for her help to make one large report into two volumes.

Although the terms of our interviews and tabletop exercises prevent us from thanking all the participants individually, we are deeply grateful for their input, thoughts, and comments. Without your contributions, this research would not have been possible. Finally, we thank Maria Falvo for her administrative assistance and Matt Byrd for coordinating the report's production.

Summary

The U.S. Department of Defense (DoD) has devoted increased attention to two critical topics: strategic competition with Russia and China and the importance of information and the information environment (IE). However, the intersection of these two areas of concern— that is, the conduct of operations in the IE (OIE) at the competition end of the continuum of conflict—has not received nearly as much focus.

There is little guidance on how the United States should organize for competition—this uncertainty is compounded by disagreements about what competition entails and how to respond appropriately when adversaries compete in the gray zone below the threshold of conflict. This report addresses these gaps by highlighting points of disagreement and synthesizing expert consensus on the implications of strategic competition for DoD, the challenges to mounting an effective response to adversaries' activities in the gray zone, and solutions to improve the U.S. competitive posture in general and in the IE specifically.[1]

Study Methods and Approach

To better define the characteristics and activities of strategic competition and how it relates to OIE, we conducted a comprehensive review of the scholarly and policy literature, as well as joint concepts and doctrine related to competition and OIE. We also conducted interviews with stakeholders and subject-matter experts to collect insights that informed our synthesis of consensus challenges and solutions, as well as our enumeration and categorization of gray zone activities in support of competition. A second component of this study involved a series of tabletop exercises with OIE practitioners, the results of which were provided to the sponsor to improve command and control for OIE and promote greater integration and coordination with joint, interagency, international, and multinational partners.

Strategic Competition

The literature and thinking on competition remain complicated and contested. For example, we found dozens of terms used in the literature to describe our subject of inquiry. None of those terms has unambiguously won the lexical fight, so we opted to use the latest language popular in guidance documents and terms used in previous RAND Corporation research, such as *strategic competition*, *competition*, and *great-power competition* to frame the overall

---

[1] This study focused on OIE during competition, but it is important to note that OIE are a foundational part of military operations across the spectrum, from cooperation to competition to conflict, and that they play a critical role in major combat operations.

topic, *gray zone* to describe the competitive context short of overt hostilities, and *gray zone activities* to describe efforts undertaken as part of strategic competition.

Although the literature has not yet reached consensus on which terms to use to describe competition, several themes appear repeatedly or otherwise imply common understanding of certain concepts:

- There is a spectrum or continuum of conflict in the context of competition.
- Thresholds are important in thinking about competition.
- Ambiguity is an inherent characteristic of competition, and it complicates strategic competition.
- Strategic competition draws on all types of national power (diplomatic, information, military, and economic).
- Competition can be conceived as a series of games.
- The logics of competition include deterrence, compellence, assurance, and inducement.

Challenges

Synthesizing the literature, we found that the nature of competition and the characteristics of the contemporary competitive environment pose several challenges for DoD and the United States more broadly. We found several challenges to be central to great-power competition or particularly salient to OIE:

- Strategic competition is fundamentally a long game between revisionist powers and those that want to preserve the status quo of the current international order. Rather than engaging in isolated contests, competitors undertake activities to gain an advantage in pursuit of one of these long-term goals.
- Strategic competition blurs the line between peace and war and occurs on a spectrum that runs from cooperation through competition and to conflict of varying intensities. The blurring of these thresholds can complicate decisions about how to respond appropriately to a competitor's actions.
- Ambiguity and uncertainty are enablers of gray zone aggression. It is difficult to mount a response when it is unclear what action has occurred and who is responsible.
- Strategic competition uses all elements of national power: diplomatic, information, military, and economic. When competing in the gray zone, states often respond to an activity related to one element of national power by harnessing an entirely different element of national power, as when military incursions are met with economic sanctions.

Possible Solutions

In addition to profiling challenges, the literature and our interviews offered several solutions to improve the U.S. competitive posture and optimize OIE for strategic competition:

- Ensure that the appropriate authorities and permissions are in place for the United States to maintain advantages in strategic competition and to compete effectively with adversaries in the gray zone. A whole-of-government approach to competition will improve coordination and progress toward U.S. goals.
- Adopt a campaigning mindset and view of adversary activities and U.S. response options as part of a competitive long game rather than discrete events. To better support this long-term vision and protect mutual interests, strengthen relationships with partners and allies and enlist their capabilities.
- Fight ambiguity with transparency. Adversaries thrive in the gray zone when it is difficult to decipher their activities or assign attribution. "Naming and shaming" is one way to disrupt this kind of incremental aggression.
- Be proactive rather than reactive, maintain a robust forward presence, and increase the risk tolerance of U.S. political and military leaders. Strategic competition has historically benefited revisionist states by putting the United States in a reactive position.
- Take a multipronged approach to managing competitors by harnessing all elements of national power in mounting a response (diplomatic, information, military, and economic), increase adversaries' costs to compete by overextending their capabilities and limiting their response options, and empower civil society institutions in partner countries to reject adversaries' information campaigns before they can have their intended effect.

Conclusions

There is no broadly shared understanding of *competition*, and there are multiple ways to conceptualize or bucket competition-related activities. However, there is consensus on the most salient challenges that the United States faces in organizing for strategic competition, competing in the gray zone, and improving coordination across the U.S. government and with allies and partners. These challenges point directly to a set of actionable solutions to leverage OIE and strengthen the U.S. competitive posture.

Contents

Tables

CHAPTER ONE

Introduction and Background

When it comes to competing effectively with Russia and China, two topics have garnered increased attention and concern in the U.S. Department of Defense (DoD):

1. the dynamics of competition, the characteristics of strategic competition, activities in the competition "gray zone," and operations below the level of large-scale combat, as well as the terminology used to discuss competition
2. the importance of information and the information environment (IE) in the context of competition, evidenced by the addition of *information* to the list of joint functions, the new joint concept for operating in the IE, and various information-focused initiatives at the service level (e.g., the creation of a deputy commandant for information in the Marine Corps, a new functional area and additional formations in the Air Force, proposed new information concepts and organizations in the Army).[1]

There is little guidance on how the United States should organize for competition—this uncertainty is compounded by disagreements about what competition entails and how to respond appropriately when adversaries compete in the gray zone below the threshold of conflict. This report addresses these gaps by highlighting points of disagreement and synthesizing expert consensus on the implications of strategic competition for DoD, the challenges to mounting an effective response to adversaries' activities in the gray zone, and solutions to improve the U.S. competitive posture in general and in the IE specifically.

Because U.S. European Command (USEUCOM) was the sponsor of this research, this report focuses on challenges, threats, and a competitive context that are specific to the European theater. However, the study's results should be applicable to other geographic combatant commands to the extent that they share similar responsibilities and face similar challenges.

---

[1] Joint Publication (JP) 1, *Doctrine for the Armed Forces of the United States*, Washington, D.C.: U.S. Joint Chiefs of Staff, incorporating change 1, July 12, 2017; DoD, *Joint Concept for Operating in the Information Environment (JCOIE)*, Washington, D.C., July 25, 2018; Mark Pomerleau, "Marines Look to Dominate in Information Environment," *C4ISRNET*, April 5, 2017; Trevor Tiernan, "First Class of Information Operations Airmen Completes 14F Initial Skills Training Course," Sixteenth Air Force (Air Forces Cyber), December 17, 2020.

Strategic Competition

The current world order is based on rules and norms that were put in place following World War II. This system is backed by assumptions and assurances that actions have consequences and that states should behave in a certain fashion, eschewing other possible actions. Various peer or near-peer competitors, revisionist powers, nonstate actors, violent extremist groups, and others are challenging this order and its proponents, the United States and the world's industrialized democracies.

Competition is not new in international relations. All states seek to both protect and advance their own interests to gain a strategic advantage.[2] Many describe the current context as a return to an era of *great-power competition* because the principal challenges to the rule-based order are coming from powerful revisionist states: the People's Republic of China and the Russian Federation.[3] The goal in competition is for nations to place themselves in positions of advantage relative to their competitors by using all elements of national power—diplomatic, military, economic, and, perhaps most importantly, information. From a military perspective, advantage is not the only objective. Rather, the goal is much broader: to deny strategic advantages to an adversary while simultaneously pursing one's own interests.[4]

Although there has been much thinking and debate on the nature of competition, various views persist, and the topic remains poorly understood. However competition is conceived or interpreted, U.S. adversaries and competitors will continue to employ a wide range of conventional and unconventional capabilities—military and otherwise—to pursue their objectives, with many operating below the thresholds that would prompt an armed response from the United States.[5] DoD must be prepared to lead or support U.S. responses to those challenges.

Competition and Operations in the Information Environment

Adding to the complexity of the competitive environment is the explosion of the internet, the Internet of Things, and social media. Today, anyone can convey information instantaneously around the globe using a plethora of platforms and channels. This explosion in communication technology has provided adversaries and competitors with easy access to the citizens of other countries and wide-open avenues for potential influence. Examples abound of competitors seeking to influence elections, spread COVID-19 disinformation, or provoke antagonism

---

[2] Joint Doctrine Note 1-19, *Competition Continuum*, Washington, D.C.: U.S. Joint Chiefs of Staff, June 3, 2019, p. 1.

[3] Defense Science Board, *2019 DSB Summer Study on the Future of U.S. Military Superiority*, Washington, D.C., June 2020, p. iii.

[4] DoD, *Summary of the Irregular Warfare Annex to the National Defense Strategy*, Washington, D.C., 2020, p. 4.

[5] U.S. Joint Chiefs of Staff, *Joint Concept for Integrated Campaigning*, Washington, D.C., March 16, 2018.

on both sides of a contentious issue (such as race, gun policy, abortion, vaccine safety, and immigration). The ever-expanding IE provides nearly boundless space for competition.

How information is harnessed to advance competition differs in several ways from how other elements of national power are used (diplomatic, economic, and military). Most relevant to the goal of our study is how competition in the IE differs from action in the traditional spatial military domains. Unlike land, sea, air, and space, the IE is not a physical place that can be visited, although it has a physical dimension (the hardware that processes, stores, transmits, and receives information, such as computers, mobile devices, servers, and routers).[6] The physical dimension of the IE can sometimes be a target, with adversaries destroying equipment or physically interrupting the flow of data. However, as articulated in prior RAND Corporation research, targets are more often "human perceptions or behaviors: Weapons are ideas, and defenses are norms, beliefs, and traditions." The implications for operations in the information environment (OIE) are clear: "If we think of conflict as requiring both the means and the will to engage the enemy, the domains of warfare are primarily concerned with means, while the IE is primarily concerned with influencing the will to act."[7]

The effective use of OIE will play a central role in U.S. efforts to counteract and compete with revisionist powers, like Russia and China. Although shaping adversaries' and competitors' perceptions and denying their objectives in pursuit of national interests is not a new phenomenon, RAND research has previously recommended that DoD "make changes across doctrine, processes, education and training, and tactics, techniques, and procedures to appropriately emphasize the importance of OIE and the role of OIE in combined arms and multidomain operations."[8] OIE in competition and conflict scenarios add additional layers of complexity to this challenge.

This project focused on the intersection of OIE and competition, but it is important to note that OIE remain a foundational component of military activity across the spectrum of conflict, from cooperation to competition and, especially, conflict. The kinetic focus of contemporary U.S. military culture makes it easy to forget that information and OIE are essential to combat operations; as a result, OIE can become consigned to a subset of operations focused on civilians or irregular combatants.[9]

---

[6] See the description of the IE in JP 3-13, *Information Operations*, Washington, D.C.: U.S. Joint Chiefs of Staff, incorporating change 1, November 20, 2014.

[7] Christopher Paul, Colin P. Clarke, Bonnie L. Triezenberg, David Manheim, and Bradley Wilson, *Improving C2 and Situational Awareness for Operations in and Through the Information Environment*, Santa Monica, Calif.: RAND Corporation, RR-2489-OSD, 2018, p. 3.

[8] Paul, Clarke, Triezenberg, et al., 2018, p. xx.

[9] Christopher Paul, Yuna Huh Wong, and Elizabeth M. Bartels, *Opportunities for Including the Information Environment in U.S. Marine Corps Wargames*, Santa Monica, Calif.: RAND Corporation, RR-2997-USMC, 2020.

The challenges addressed in this report also have implications at the conflict end of the spectrum, particularly at the seam between competition and conflict.[10] It is here that OIE move away from a steady-state competitive focus on, for example, narrative, counterpropaganda, deterrence and signaling, and setting conditions favorable to friendly forces to a focus on wartime missions, such as undermining enemy will to fight, interfering with adversary leaders' decisionmaking and command and control (C2), and concealing the plans and presence of friendly forces.

Study Methods and Approach

The goal of this research was to support continued conceptual development related to competition, with an emphasis on OIE. To better define the characteristics and activities of strategic competition and how it relates to OIE, we conducted a comprehensive review of the scholarly and policy literature, as well as joint concepts and doctrine related to competition and OIE. We also conducted interviews with stakeholders and subject-matter experts (SMEs) to collect insights that informed our synthesis of consensus challenges and solutions, as well as our enumeration and categorization of gray zone activities in support of competition.

A second component of this study involved a series of tabletop exercises with OIE practitioners, the results of which were provided to the sponsor to inform potential organizational changes to improve C2 for OIE and to promote greater integration and coordination with joint, interagency, international, and multinational partners.

Literature Review

This report builds on a larger body of RAND research. As such, we considered important prior RAND work related to competition and OIE, as well as a range of academic studies, military doctrine, and concepts on these themes.

One of the goals of the literature review was to populate the lists of gray zone activities presented in Chapter Three, which was part of our process to refine our characterization of strategic competition and to identify activities that are relevant to OIE in the context of competition. To build these lists, each team member independently identified and collected potentially relevant materials and compiled a list of candidate activities, which we then synthesized into a single master list. We approached the review in this way to ensure that we cast a wide net and as a form of cross-validation; if team members produced substantially similar lists, we had higher confidence in the entries. Making each team member responsible for an independent initial list (rather than asking them to contribute to a group list) also mitigated the risk of groupthink or free-rider incentives to make minimal additions to an initial contribution by a diligent colleague.

---

[10] Paul, Clarke, Triezenberg, et al., 2018.

This initial effort produced 445 individual entries across 23 topic areas. There was substantial redundancy across the lists (a good thing from a cross-validation perspective). After combining, distilling, and synthesizing the entries, we identified 110 specific activities in 17 categories. These activities and categories are presented in Tables 3.1–3.5 in Chapter Three.

Stakeholder and SME Interviews

Stakeholder and SME interviews also supported the project's lines of inquiry. Given the substantial body of RAND research related to competition, we began with internal consultations with RAND researchers who had worked on those studies. We also spoke with numerous DoD stakeholders and SMEs identified through our prior research and professional experience in this area, as well as suggestions from the sponsor and referrals from the interviewees themselves (i.e., "Who else should we speak to about this important topic?"). Through our internal interviews, we learned that a parallel RAND project for the U.S. Army was exploring interagency policymaking and coordination processes related to strategic competition. We arranged to add a few topics addressed in that study to our semistructured interview protocol and arranged to share interview notes with that research team. In that way, both research teams were able to assemble a larger corpus of interviews, and we avoided overburdening SMEs with expertise that was relevant to both projects.

Table 1.1 lists the organizations represented in this corpus of interviews and the number of personnel who participated from each organization. This is not a representative sample tied to a known population, so we undertook no quantitative analyses of the interview responses; we present the numbers simply to note that we, in concert with the other project team, spoke to a large number of SMEs and stakeholders from a variety of relevant organizations.

Organization of This Report

The remainder of this report unfolds in five additional chapters. Chapter Two explores differing views on competition and distills points of expert consensus on essential concepts, logics, and goals of strategic competition. Chapter Three enumerates core activities related to competition, organized according to the elements of national power that they employ, with a particularly extensive review of activities in the IE. Chapter Four features an overview of challenges to OIE in the context of competition that we identified in our literature review, while Chapter Five presents promising solutions to address those challenges. Chapter Six concludes this report with general observations and suggestions for further research on these themes to better integrate OIE and support a stronger U.S. competitive posture.

TABLE 1.1

Numbers and Organizational Affiliations of Interview Participants

Organization	Number of Interviewees
U.S. Army (Headquarters, U.S. Department of the Army; U.S. Army Europe; U.S. Army Pacific; Army Materiel Command; Army Human Resources Command; Army National Guard; Army Civil Affairs)	19
Office of the Secretary of Defense (OSD)	11
Joint organizations (Joint Staff, Joint Interagency Task Force–South, Joint Information Operations Warfare Center)	9
Defense agencies (Defense Security Cooperation Agency, Defense Logistics Agency)	2
Geographic and functional combatant commands (USEUCOM, U.S. Indo-Pacific Command, U.S. Cyber Command)	6
National Security Council (current and former members)	2
U.S. Department of State	7
U.S. Agency for International Development	1
North Atlantic Treaty Organization (NATO) headquarters	4
Private sector (Center for European Policy Analysis, Wilson Center)	2
RAND Corporation	18
Total	81

CHAPTER TWO

Differing Views and Consensus on Competition

DoD is rightly focused on strategic competition, but there is a lack of consensus surrounding the appropriate terms to describe, characterize, and bound competition. Likewise, there is uncertainty regarding the role of OIE and various elements of the U.S. government in the context of competition. However, there is expert consensus on some of the dynamics of competition too. Drawing on these debates and points of agreement, this chapter explores the competition lexicon, distills central concepts, enumerates core activities of competition (with an emphasis on OIE), and highlights both challenges to conducting OIE in a competition context and attendant solutions.

In our interviews, we asked DoD personnel about how they and others interpreted *competition* and how well it was understood in their organizations. We heard many different views. Some interviewees claimed that competition was sufficiently understood and that existing guidance was adequate, but most expressed less confidence. One told us, "There are a multitude of views about competition [as to] what it is, what it should do, who it involves," adding, "Everyone brings a different starting position."[1] Another offered a particularly extreme view: "No one knows what competition is."[2] This ambiguity, lack of understanding, and lack of consensus can be an impediment to implementing a coherent strategy and promoting unity of effort within DoD.[3]

Given a baseline of disagreement and uncertainty about the nature of competition, it was unsurprising that interviewees also expressed uncertainty regarding DoD's assigned and appropriate roles when it came to competition. One interviewee captured the contours of both uncertainty about the nature of competition and uncertainty about DoD's role:

> There is no really clear definition of what competition is, and we're not sure what [our] specific roles are. We recognize that competition is a whole-of-government effort, but we do not have a clear understanding to move forward aggressively. There is no clear delineation of roles and missions. The [National Defense Strategy] frames it and says [the DoD

---

[1] Semistructured interview with an OSD official, May 8, 2020.

[2] Semistructured interview with a Joint Staff (J5) official, May 21, 2020.

[3] Semistructured interview with an OSD official, May 8, 2020.

role] is to compete, deter, win [and then focuses] more on deter and win. With that in mind, if we take this mindset, anything short of that is not in the DoD purview, but this is not a really good perspective.[4]

Others noted that although DoD's role is not clear, commands have been instructed to "get out there and compete."[5] One official described the absence of a joint operating concept for competition, similar to the existing joint concept for deterrence, and the resulting uncertainty around how the joint force should prepare for competition.[6] Another noted that the idea of ongoing competition without clear and specific end states is "hard for military people to grasp."[7] In addition, interviewees emphasized there is no process in place to properly assess U.S. competition with adversaries, including how to measure success.[8]

Interviewees' disparate views and uncertainty surrounding competition echoed the current state of the scholarly and policy literature. RAND colleagues have noted that "while there is a general expectation of a new era of strategic competition, there is not yet clear understanding what that means, what forms it could take, and what it might imply for U.S. national security or U.S. defense policy."[9] Rising in intensity in the 2014–2015 period, and with an intellectual pedigree dating back to the Cold War, discussions and disagreements about the terms that could or should be used to characterize strategic competition have not abated.

Terminology

The box on the following page lists the terms we encountered in our review of the literature that were used to describe competition or something like it; sources for the terms are noted in footnotes. A brief discussion of particularly interesting (or contested) terms follows. Without prejudice or enduring commitment to these specific terms, in this report, we use *strategic competition*, *competition*, or *great-power competition* to frame the overall topic, *gray zone* to describe the competitive context short of overt hostilities, and *gray zone activities* to describe the efforts that nations undertake (or have undertaken on their behalf) as part of strategic competition. Discussing the history, definitions, and related debates around these terms would require several pages each, so we do not offer detailed descriptions but instead highlight example sources from our literature review that define and contextualize the terms.

---

4 Semistructured interview with OSD official, May 18, 2020.

5 Semistructured interview with a Joint Staff (J5) official, May 21, 2020.

6 Semistructured interview with a U.S. Cyber Command official, June 5, 2020.

7 Semistructured interview with an OSD official, May 18, 2020.

8 Semistructured interviews with a Joint Staff (J7) official, May 15, 2020; Joint Staff (J5) official, May 21, 2020; and U.S. Army Pacific (G-39) official, May 5, 2020.

9 Michael J. Mazarr, Jonathan Blake, Abigail Casey, Tim McDonald, Stephanie Pezard, and Michael Spirtas, *Understanding the Emerging Era of International Competition: Theoretical and Historical Perspectives*, Santa Monica, Calif.: RAND Corporation, RR-2726-AF, 2018, p. 2.

Terms Related to Competition

Active measures	Gray zone	Noncontact warfare
Ambiguous warfare	Gray zone tactics	Nonlinear warfare
Asymmetrical warfare	Hostile social manipulation	Noopolitik
Coercive gradualism	Hostile measures	Political warfare
Competition	Hybrid warfare	Proxy warfare
Conflict	Hypercompetition	Rivalry
Constrained military operations	Irregular warfare	Salami-slicing
Contestation	Measures short of war	Unconventional warfare
Escalation dominance	Next-generation warfare	Unrestricted warfare
Fait accompli	New-generation warfare	Wars of influence
Full-spectrum warfare		

SOURCES: Ben Connable, Stephanie Young, Stephanie Pezard, Andrew Radin, Raphael S. Cohen, Katya Migacheva, and James Sladden, *Russia's Hostile Measures: Combating Russian Gray Zone Aggression Against NATO in the Contact, Blunt, and Surge Layers of Competition*, Santa Monica, Calif.: RAND Corporation, RR-2539-A, 2020; Mary Ellen Connell and Ryan Evans, *Russia's "Ambiguous Warfare" and Implications for the U.S. Marine Corps*, Arlington, Va.: CNA, May 2015; Anthony H. Cordesman and Grace Hwang, *The Biden Transition and U.S. Competition with China and Russia: The Crisis-Driven Need to Change U.S. Strategy*, Washington, D.C.: Center for Strategic and International Studies, January 6, 2021; Richard A. Curtis, "Contemporary Warfare Model—A Conceptual Framework of Modern Warfare," U.S. Air Force Special Operations School, undated; Defense Science Board, *Summer Study on Capabilities for Constrained Military Operations*, Washington, D.C., December 2016; Adam Elkus, "Abandon All Hope, Ye Who Enter Here: You Cannot Save the Gray Zone Concept," *War on the Rocks*, December 30, 2015; Nate Freier, James Hayes, Michael Hatfield, and Lisa Lamb, "Game On or Game Over: Hypercompetition and Military Advantage," *War Room*, May 22, 2018; Frank G. Hoffman, *Conflict in the 21st Century: The Rise of Hybrid Wars*, Arlington, Va.: Potomac Institute for Policy Studies, December 2007; Frank G. Hoffman, "Hybrid Warfare and Challenges," *Joint Force Quarterly*, No. 52, First Quarter 2009; Frank Hoffman, "Sharpening Our Military Edge: The NDS and the Full Continuum of Conflict," *Small Wars Journal*, June 27, 2018; Phillip Karber and Joshua Thibeault, "Russia's New-Generation Warfare," Association of the United States Army, May 20, 2016; George Kennan, *The Inauguration of Organized Political Warfare*, declassified archival document, Washington, D.C.: U.S. Department of State Policy Planning Staff, April 30, 1948a; Michael J. Mazarr, *Mastering the Gray Zone: Understanding a Changing Era of Conflict*, Carlisle Barracks, Pa.: U.S. Army War College Press, December 2015; Michael J. Mazarr, Abigail Casey, Alyssa Demus, Scott W. Harold, Luke J. Matthews, Nathan Beauchamp-Mustafaga, and James Sladden, *Hostile Social Manipulation: Present Realities and Emerging Trends*, Santa Monica, Calif.: RAND Corporation, RR-2713-OSD, 2019; Mazarr et al., 2018; Stacie L. Pettyjohn and Becca Wasser, *Competing in the Gray Zone: Russian Tactics and Western Responses*, Santa Monica, Calif.: RAND Corporation, RR-2791-A, 2019; William G. Pierce, Douglas G. Douds, and Michael A. Marra, "Countering Gray-Zone Wars: Understanding Coercive Gradualism," *Parameters*, Vol. 45, No. 3, Autumn 2015; Peter Pomerantsev, "Brave New War: A New Form of Conflict Emerged in 2015—From the Islamic State to the South China Sea," *The Atlantic*, December 29, 2015; David Ronfeldt and John Arquilla, *Whose Story Wins: Rise of the Noosphere, Noopolitik, and Information-Age Statecraft*, Santa Monica, Calif.: RAND Corporation, PE-A237-1, 2020; Thomas C. Schelling, *Arms and Influence*, New Haven, Conn.: Yale University Press, 1966; U.S. Army Special Operations Command, *SOF Support to Political Warfare*, white paper, Fort Bragg, N.C., March 10, 2015; U.S. Special Operations Command, *The Gray Zone*, white paper, Washington, D.C., September 9, 2015.

For efficiency, we limit the remainder of this discussion to consensus points and key characteristics distilled from the literature, focusing first on terminology and then on concepts in the next section.

Despite its numerous definitions, *gray zone* appears to be winning the lexical battle in that it both clearly captures many of the most salient characteristics of competition and is the most frequently used term to describe competition-related challenges and concepts. However, one of the most common criticisms is it does not actually describe anything new or anything that is adequately covered by existing terms, such as *salami-slicing* or *political warfare*.[10] RAND colleagues seeking to sidestep the debate have noted that much of the criticism of *gray zone* focuses on the term's use to refer to a type or phase of a conflict or as context for competition; instead, they conceptualized *gray zone* as a category of activities or a set of tactics that share some characteristics.[11]

The box also includes several terms with the word *warfare*.[12] One of the hallmarks of consensus views on strategic competition is that it occurs in a competitive space short of open conflict and focuses equally or more on political and economic contestation than on military efforts. This has led to criticism that it is oxymoronic to refer to *competition* as any flavor of warfare.[13] In the broader category of warfare terms, *hybrid warfare* is one of the earliest terminological contestants and also subject to a great deal of criticism—in part because the term and its definitions have relatively poor overlap with contemporary conceptions of strategic competition.[14] Briefly, *hybrid warfare*, as introduced in the literature, typically referred to the simultaneous employment of conventional and unconventional forces or operations rather than the intentional exploitation of the space between peace and war.

Essential Concepts

The terms and ideas in the academic and policy literature on competition are diverse and conceptually rich. In this section, we present support for consensus concepts (to the extent that they exist) in the literature. In formulating this discussion, we looked for recurring themes and concepts that captured something essential about competition in an attempt tie together existing and emerging points of consensus in the literature.

---

[10] See, for example, Elkus, 2015.

[11] Pettyjohn and Wasser, 2019.

[12] They are *asymmetrical warfare, full-spectrum warfare, hybrid warfare, irregular warfare, next-generation warfare, new-generation warfare, noncontact warfare, nonlinear warfare, political warfare, proxy warfare, unconventional warfare*, and *unrestricted warfare*.

[13] Frank Hoffman, "On Not-So-New Warfare: Political Warfare vs Hybrid Threats," *War on the Rocks*, July 28, 2014.

[14] Nadia Schadlow, "The Problem with Hybrid Warfare," *War on the Rocks*, April 2, 2015; Samuel Charap, "The Ghost of Hybrid Warfare," *Survival*, Vol. 57, No. 6, 2015; Christopher Paul, "Confessions of a Hybrid Warfare Skeptic: What Might Really Be Interesting but Hidden Within the Various Conceptions of Gray Zone Conflict, Ambiguous Warfare, Political Warfare, and Their Ilk," *Small Wars Journal*, March 3, 2016.

There Is a Spectrum or Continuum of Conflict and Competition

The first consensus concept worth highlighting is that strategic competition blurs the line between peace and war and takes place on a spectrum that runs from cooperation through competition and to conflicts of varying intensities.[15] This is not a new concept. In his 1948 policy memorandum, George Kennan called for U.S. leadership to shed the view that there is a "basic difference between peace and war."[16] Similar declarations are common in the contemporary competition literature, including in a 2015 U.S. Special Operations Command white paper and in the Joint Concept for Integrated Campaigning.[17]

Thresholds Are Important in Thinking About Competition

Related to the continuum of competition is the concept of thresholds. Building on the notion of a false dichotomy between war and peace, aggression during competition is often explicitly designed to stay under the threshold of war.[18] Great-power competition hinges on revisionist powers seeking to change some aspect of the international order without resorting to war or provoking a response that escalates to war.[19] Moreover, gray zone aggression sometimes seeks to remain under the threshold of *perception*, where one party to the competition is unaware that change is taking place.[20]

Important to the understanding of these thresholds is that they are somewhat fluid and dynamic. They might appear to be clear "red lines" that, if crossed will automatically prompt a response and escalation, but in practice "threshold stretching" or "threshold exploitation" is frequently part of gray zone aggression. RAND colleagues have defined *threshold stretching* as "applying measures short of war to force movement or change in the nature of a threshold to gain greater regional influence, access, and control" and *threshold exploitation* as "taking advantage of a competitor's inability to enforce or miscalculation of a declared or tacit threshold for high-order war."[21] Importantly, OIE are almost always viewed as being insufficiently provocative to cross a threshold; because of this ambiguity, such operations are often carried out below the threshold of perception—or at least below the threshold of attribution.

---

[15] U.S. Joint Chiefs of Staff, 2018.

[16] George Kennan, "Policy Planning Memorandum," declassified archival document, Washington, D.C.: U.S. Department of State Policy Planning Staff, May 4, 1948b.

[17] U.S. Special Operations Command, 2015; U.S. Joint Chiefs of Staff, 2018.

[18] See, for example, U.S. Joint Chiefs of Staff, 2018, and U.S. Army Training and Doctrine Command, *Multi-Domain Battle: Evolution of Combined Arms for the 21st Century 2025–2040*, version 1.0, Fort Eustis, Va., December 2017.

[19] Hal Brands, "Paradoxes of the Gray Zone," Foreign Policy Research Institute, February 5, 2016.

[20] Schadlow, 2015; Paul, 2016.

[21] Ben Connable, Jason H. Campbell, and Dan Madden, *Stretching and Exploiting Thresholds for High-Order War: How Russia, China, and Iran Are Eroding American Influence Using Time-Tested Measures Short of War*, Santa Monica, Calif.: RAND Corporation, RR-1003-A, 2016, p. ix.

Ambiguity Complicates Strategic Competition

There is consensus in the competition literature on the concept of ambiguity, how it allows an actor to avoid detection or a reaction, and how it provides opportunities to stretch or exploit thresholds. This shared understanding is even reflected in doctrine, with Marine Corps Doctrinal Publication 1-4, *Competing*, emphasizing the role of ambiguity, uncertainty, and boundary-stretching in competition.[22]

Ambiguity is the central characteristic of gray zone challenges, and it is the impetus for the *gray* in the term itself. Gray zone activities are often shrouded in deception and conducted in ways that create ambiguity about what is happening and who is responsible.[23] Even where the actions and actors are clear, the purpose or intent might be concealed or misrepresented.[24] In other cases, gray zone activities, actors, and intents might be clear but merely fit within the seams of thresholds for response (e.g., blurring the line between legality and illegality), prompting uncertainty about who should take a counteraction, paralyzing decision-making, and confusing public opinion.[25] An example is the maritime aggression of China's coast guard, which is notionally a law enforcement entity.[26] Creeping incremental aggression and sustained uncertainty about what is being done and whether it merits a response allow gray zone activities to "eat away at the status quo one nibble at a time."[27] Classic literature on deception refers to *ambiguity increasing* as one of the two main types of deception, and deception is an OIE capability.[28] Competitors intentionally seek to create ambiguity around their actions to gain advantages in competition and complicate other competitors' responses.

Strategic Competition Uses All Types of National Power

One of the reasons for the variation in the terms and definitions related to competition is the range of capabilities and types of power involved. When it comes to the gray zone, Peter Pomerantsev has said, "variations in the description indicate the slipperiness of the subject—these conflicts mix psychological, media, economic, cyber, and military operations without

---

[22] Marine Corps Doctrinal Publication 1-4, *Competing*, Washington, D.C.: Headquarters, U.S. Marine Corps, December 2020.

[23] Brands, 2016.

[24] U.S. Joint Chiefs of Staff, 2018.

[25] U.S. Joint Chiefs of Staff, 2018.

[26] Cleo Paskal, "Protection from China's Comprehensive National Power Requires Comprehensive National Defence," Kalinga Institute of Indo-Pacific Studies, September 2, 2020.

[27] The quote is from Brands, 2016; see also Lyle J. Morris, Michael J. Mazarr, Jeffrey W. Hornung, Stephanie Pezard, Anika Binnendijk, and Marta Kepe, *Gaining Competitive Advantage in the Gray Zone: Response Options for Coercive Aggression Below the Threshold of Major War*, Santa Monica, Calif.: RAND Corporation, RR-2942-OSD, 2019.

[28] Zell Stanley, *An Annotated Bibliography of the Open Literature on Deception*, Santa Monica, Calif.: RAND Corporation, N-2332-NA, 1985.

requiring a declaration of war."[29] The consensus is that strategic competition and gray zone aggression can not only mix a range of military capabilities from conventional to irregular but also use all elements of national power: diplomatic, informational, military, and economic.[30]

Competition Can Be Conceived as a Series of Games

Elements of game theory are not uncommon in discussions about strategic competition. There is some debate about whether competition is always zero-sum (that is, one competitor achieving an objective requires a corresponding loss by another) or whether it can be positive-sum (every competitor can gain, but not necessarily equally). Other thinkers draw contrasts between finite and infinite games, wherein the former has a clear end and outcome, while the latter has neither.[31] A good example is American football. A single football game is a finite game, with a fixed time of play and an outcome that is a win for one team, a loss for the other, and very rarely a draw. Even the National Football League season is finite and could be considered a single, lengthy game: After the regular season games, a predetermined number of playoff games, and the Super Bowl, teams return for a new season with the same 0-0 records. But, the entire National Football League could still be viewed as an infinite game. Teams continue competing to maintain their rosters of players and their fan base. Each team is a business that seeks to remain viable in the next season and the one after that. Done right, there is no "end" to the league; it persists, and plays, in perpetuity.

Competition has characteristics of both finite and infinite games. Think of strategic competition as an endless series (an infinite game) of contests (finite games), some of which are zero-sum, some of which are positive-sum, some of which are played only once, and some of which are played again and again. In this endless series of games, a wily competitor will avoid playing games at which they are disadvantaged. This ability to choose which games to initiate is to the aggressor's advantage in strategic competition and favors revisionist powers over those burdened with enforcing the status quo: Declining to initiate a game preserves the status quo, but initiating a game in which you have an advantage (or can use subterfuge or ambiguity to create an advantage) increases your odds of winning that finite game and progressing toward revisionist goals.

References to games and game theory imply rules, and breaking rules (or norms) is a hallmark of gray zone aggression. After all, "competition implies rules, for one thing, which Moscow and Beijing don't accept."[32]

---

[29] Pomerantsev, 2015.

[30] Cordesman and Hwang, 2021.

[31] Jen Judson, "The Infinite Game: How the U.S. Army Plans to Operate in Great Power Competition," *Defense News*, March 29, 2021.

[32] Sydney J. Freedberg, Jr., "US Needs New Strategy to Combat Russian, Chinese 'Political Warfare': CSBA," *Breaking Defense*, May 31, 2018, p. 1. Also see Anthony H. Cordesman and Grace Hwang, *Chronology of Possible Chinese Gray Area and Hybrid Warfare Operations*, working draft, Washington, D.C.: Center for Strategic and International Studies, September 28, 2020.

There is consensus that there are no fixed rules in international competition and that this is also to the advantage of revisionist powers. Importantly, some thinkers acknowledge that although the rules are not fixed, even strongly revisionist powers are bound by *some* rules. There is some normative force at work here: If international norms did not affect competition, revisionist powers would not be spending so much energy seeking to change them. And when competitors act outside of broadly accepted norms, they do so at their peril. Both China and Russia have faced considerable opprobrium in response to their normative violations, and it remains to be seen whether their material gains will outweigh the losses associated with the reputational damage.

Finally, competitors are constrained by the rules of their own self-identities.[33] Culture and identity still shape nations, their leaders, and how their leaders approach competition: What kind of situation is this? What kind of nation are we? What might a nation like us do in a situation like this? The rules implicit in those answers will differ, but they still provide structure to strategic competition.

Logics of Competition

Not all scholarly and policy discussions related to competition explicitly examine the logics or mechanisms that connect gray zone activities to objectives. However, there are clear themes in those that do. Table 2.1 captures the core logic enumerated in Blechman and Kaplan's 1978 classic *Force Without War*, noting four logics: deterrence, compellence, assurance, and inducement.[34]

Beyond (and sometimes related or subordinate to) Blechman and Kaplan's four logics, there are other terms. For example, Marine Corps Doctrinal Publication 1-4 mentions *attraction*, which could contribute to either assurance or inducement.[35] *Coercion* is just an umbrella

TABLE 2.1
Logics of Behavior Change in *Force Without War*

Influence on Behavior by a Friendly Actor	Influence on Behavior by a Hostile Actor	
	Reinforce	Modify
Reinforce	Deterrence	Compellence
Modify	Assurance	Inducement

SOURCE: Abstracted from Blechman and Kaplan, 1978.

---

[33] Mazarr et al., 2018, p. 1.

[34] Barry M. Blechman and Stephen S. Kaplan, *Force Without War: U.S. Armed Forces as a Political Instrument*, Washington, D.C.: Brookings Institution, 1978.

[35] Marine Corps Doctrinal Publication 1-4, 2020.

term for both compellence and deterrence, while *dissuasion* is a synonym for deterrence. Cost-imposing or cost-raising can be part of either deterrence or compellence.[36]

The Joint Concept for Integrated Campaigning lists several mechanisms that would probably fit comfortably in Table 2.2: improve, counter, contest, engage, maintain, advance, strengthen, create, preserve, weaken, position, inform, and persuade.[37]

Goals Sought Through Competition

Synthesizing the literature, we identified the range of goals pursued through competition. Strategic competition might not end, but all competitors have ends (objectives). The first of these is somewhat tautological: One of the goals of competition is achieving (or making incremental progress toward) objectives.[38] According to Mazarr et al., states compete to pursue objectives in seven areas:

- power and security
- status, standing, and prestige
- material economic prosperity and power
- resources
- territorial or sovereign claims
- values and ideology
- the rules, norms, and institutions of the larger system.[39]

In addition, competitors can attempt to deny their opponents such gains, to preserve the status quo, or to achieve advantage. The notion of *advantage* merits further discussion.

Competitors always seek advantages, and not always as ends in themselves. The prospect of gaining an advantage can drive where and how competitors choose to compete. Thinking back to the four *Force Without War* logics, *having* an advantage can help with deterrence and assurance, while compellence and inducement require *using* or *leveraging* an advantage.

The Contemporary Competitive Environment

What are the characteristics of the contemporary competitive environment in which the United States operates? RAND colleagues have written thoughtfully on exactly this topic, and we summarize that work here, adding observations from other scholars.

---

[36] Steven Metz, "How to Deter Russia from Meddling in Democracies," *World Politics Review*, May 12, 2017.

[37] U.S. Joint Chiefs of Staff, 2018.

[38] Marine Corps Doctrinal Publication 1-4, 2020, p. 4-14.

[39] Mazarr et al., 2018, p. 1.

First, contemporary competition is not a matter of everyone competing against everyone else. It is most intensely initiated by a small number of revisionist states: Russia, China, and, to a lesser extent, North Korea and Iran.[40]

Second, contemporary competition hinges on tension between the leader and architect of the current rules-based order (the United States) and revisionists.[41] The competition is fundamentally about whose rules will win and who sets the rules going forward. The rules are at the center of the competition because of the perception that the current order is biased against revisionist powers (or at least their ambitions). Thus, the third characteristic is that contemporary competition is focused on status grievances or ambitions, economic prosperity, technological advantages, and regional influence.[42] Revisionist powers want "their due" and to be able to influence, exploit, or coerce their neighbors without interference from other powers.

Fourth, these revisionists all have governance models that ignore or do not take seriously the current rules-based order, such as the rule of law and the distinction between public and private ownership and control.[43] The domestic governance of these competitors—which can reasonably be characterized as authoritarian regimes—endow their decisionmakers with certain advantages when competing in the gray zone, such as unity of command.[44] Unified control of the levers of power is undemocratic, but it can be efficient and can streamline decisionmaking.

Fifth, aggression by revisionists makes it easier to build coalitions to respond to their aggressions.[45] Aggressive and public coercion efforts open up space for the United States to rally partners in support of each other and the rule-based order. Put another way, if the revisionists compete in ways that paint them as "bad guys," it is more likely that other countries will accept the United States in the role of "good guy."

Sixth, and finally, there is an open question about the role of the United States in the contemporary competitive environment. Some authors have argued compellingly that the United States is a status quo power, seeking to preserve the current rules-based order and international system. Indeed, many U.S. strategic objectives have to do with preservation and countering revisionist influence, with a few marginal improvements, such as extending the reach of democracy and spreading positive-sum economic, public health, and security advantages among partners. However, others have noted that many countries perceive the United States as the most highly disruptive revisionist of all.[46] What Americans think of as

---

[40] Mazarr et al., 2018, p. 1.

[41] Mazarr et al., 2018, p. 1.

[42] Mazarr et al., 2018, p. 1.

[43] Mazarr et al., 2018, p. 1.

[44] U.S. Special Operations Command, 2015.

[45] Morris et al., 2019.

[46] Mazarr et al., 2018.

Patterns in Russia's Use of Gray Zone Activities

Some features of the contemporary competitive environment identified in the literature are narrower and specific to a single revisionist power: Russia. Given that USEUCOM sponsored this research and Russia is the predominant U.S. competitor in that area of responsibility, we identified several points of consensus on Russia's approach to competition as distilled in prior RAND research. RAND colleagues summarized seven patterns in what they referred to as Russia's use of hostile measures (a synonym for what we call *gray zone activities* in this report). We repeat their list here.

1. Russia consistently reacts with hostile measures when it perceives threats.
2. Both opportunism and reactionism drive Russian behavior.
3. Russian leaders issue a public warning before employing reactive hostile measures.
4. Short- and long-term measures are applied in mutually supporting combination.
5. Diplomatic, information, military, and economic means are used collectively.
6. Russia emphasizes information, economic, and diplomatic measures, in that order.
7. All arms of the government are used to apply hostile measures, often in concert.

SOURCE: Connable et al., 2020, p. xv.

modest improvements on the status quo (the aforementioned promotion of democracy, for instance) can perhaps rightly be viewed as highly revisionist in countries where the U.S. version of democracy is promoted. Since 1945, the United States has intervened militarily in more countries than any other. As Mazarr et al. caution, "The United States will not be able to fully comprehend others' reactions to its policies in the emerging competition without taking more seriously than before its own role as global disruptor."[47]

---

[47] Mazarr et al., 2018, p. 18.

CHAPTER THREE

Enumeration and Categorization of Gray Zone Activities

So, what actions and activities do competitors undertake as part of strategic competition? As an extension of our literature review and as described in Chapter One, we sought to enumerate, distill, and categorize the types of gray zone activities that make up strategic competition.

Tables 3.1–3.5 show the gray zone activities we summarized and synthesized in the first phase of this research. The activities are sorted by the corresponding element of national power: diplomatic, informational, military, and economic. However, we have divided *military* into *unconventional* and *conventional* activities (hence there are five tables). Although this report focuses on informational power and OIE, we present the tables in "DIME" order (diplomatic, informational, military, and economic) to align with the standard approach to presenting such material. This means that OIE are not addressed until Table 3.2. Also note that gray zone actions often incorporate multiple elements of national power. Many military activities, for example, leverage informational or diplomatic power by contributing to signaling. To avoid duplicate entries across tables, we categorized the actions according to the type of power required to *undertake* them rather than the types of power mobilized as part of the actions' *effects*. Within each table, we further sorted and categorized the actions to place "like with like" and provide a clearer picture of how activities rely on a given element of national power.

Table 3.1 lists activities related to the diplomatic element of national power. These activities fall into four categories: traditional diplomatic actions; bans, embargoes, designations, and laws; cooperation; and underhanded diplomacy.

TABLE 3.1
Diplomatic Activities

Category	Diplomatic Activities
Traditional diplomatic actions	• Entering into, enforcing, modifying, or withdrawing from treaties, alliances, or trade agreements • Making, rejecting, or agreeing to various proposals (such as ceasefires) • Suspending or resuming diplomatic relations, opening or closing embassies, expelling diplomats or embassy staff, or augmenting or downsizing staff • Signaling through government spokespeople or formal protests (or demarche) from embassies; includes "naming and shaming" other countries' aggressive acts • Back-channel signaling, protest, or complaint • Facilitating or halting cultural and other exchanges

Table 3.1—Continued

Category	Diplomatic Activities
Bans, embargoes, designations, and laws or legal action	• Imposing (or lifting) economic sanctions or bans on countries, individuals, firms, or products • Designating actions (or actors) as belonging to a pejorative category through, e.g., genocide, terrorism, specially designated nationals or blocked persons lists, or lists of state sponsors of terrorism • Passing laws criminalizing certain forms of behavior (such as arms transfers between countries or spreading disinformation) or limiting foreign investment, ownership, or rights • Indicting, arresting, or prosecuting those who undertake or sponsor competitive actions that are both out of normative bounds and illegal • Immigration and migration control, including visa restrictions, revocations, or selective approvals • Boycotting international events
Cooperation	• Emphasizing legitimacy, strong social outreach, and support for inclusive policies that avoid discrimination and reduce separatism • Conducting outreach or providing financial support to partner nations, either to meet needs or encourage positive relations • Using international institutions to reassure allies, build consensus, promote allied claims, or establish norms • Working together with competitors to advance mutual interests, perhaps as a carrot to avoid aggressive forms of competition • Engaging with or legitimizing a competitor's political opposition
Underhanded diplomacy	• Implicit or explicit intimidation and threats (economic, military, legal), including seeking to cause reputation harm to prevent coercive use of power • Instituting bans or embargoes under false pretenses; agreeing to proposals with no intention of adhering to them • Claiming, annexing, or creating territory (e.g., island-building) • Passportization or creating other thin legal excuses for protest or intervention • Legitimizing one's own aggressive behavior by declaring it a response to a competitor's behavior (two wrongs make a right) • Using international institutions for either exploitation (strengthening claims, promoting self-serving rules, or creating a false appearance of consensus) or enforcement (excluding aggressor participation or censuring)

SOURCES: Analysis and synthesis of actions described in Collin Anderson and Karim Sadjadpour, *Iran's Cyber Threat: Espionage, Sabotage, and Revenge*, Washington, D.C.: Carnegie Endowment for International Peace, 2018; Connell and Evans, 2015; Cordesman and Hwang, 2021; James Dobbins, Howard J. Shatz, and Ali Wyne, *Russia Is a Rogue, Not a Peer; China Is a Peer, Not a Rogue: Different Challenges, Different Responses*, Santa Monica, Calif.: RAND Corporation, PE-310-A, 2019; Molly Dunigan, Brodi Kotila, Kimberly Jackson, Ashley L. Rhoades, and John J. Drennan, *Competing to Win: Coordinating and Leveraging U.S. Army Contributions to Strategic Competition*, Santa Monica, Calif.: RAND Corporation, RR-A718-1, forthcoming; Mark Galeotti, "Time to Think About 'Hybrid Defense,'" *War on the Rocks*, July 30, 2015; Keir Giles, "Countering Russian Information Operations in the Age of Social Media," Council on Foreign Relations, November 21, 2017; Agnia Grigas, *Beyond Crimea: The New Russian Empire*, New Haven, Conn.: Yale University Press, 2016; Kennan, 1948b; Mazarr, Casey, 2019; Mazarr, 2015; Joss Meakins, *Living in (Digital) Denial: Russia's Approach to Cyber Deterrence*, London: European Leadership Network, July 2018; Morris et al., 2019; Eric Olson, "America's Not Ready for Today's Gray Wars," *Defense One*, December 10, 2015; Bret Perry, "Non-Linear Warfare in Ukraine: The Critical Role of Information Operations and Special Operations," *Small Wars Journal*, August 14, 2015; Pettyjohn and Wasser, 2019; Schadlow, 2015; U.S. Joint Chiefs of Staff, 2018; U.S. Army Special Operations Command, *Counter-Unconventional Warfare*, white paper, Fort Bragg, N.C., September 26, 2014; Hans von der Burchard, "EU Takes Billion-Euro Battle to Russia," *Politico*, January 5, 2018; Becca Wasser, Jenny Oberholtzer, Stacie L. Pettyjohn, and William Mackenzie, *Gaming Gray Zone Tactics: Design Considerations for a Structured Strategic Game*, Santa Monica, Calif.: RAND Corporation, RR-2915-A, 2019; Brian D. Wieck, "Information Operations Countermeasures to Anti-Access/Area Denial," *Strategy Bridge*, May 11, 2017.

Table 3.2 lists activities related to the information element of national power and OIE (the aspect of competition that is the primary focus of this report). The table differs from the others in this series in that the actions that support OIE differ from those associated with other elements of national power. Information power is not confined to specific media and does not necessarily require sophisticated capabilities, so the same activities might be undertaken by a range of competitors or actors aligned with a competitor, through a range of modes and media, and for a range of purposes. Because this report focuses on OIE, we chose not to abstract these important variations and instead listed them separately. Table 3.2 begins with a categorized list of actions and then presents motivations and participants. All the actions listed at the beginning of the table could be undertaken for various purposes, by various actors, in various ways. Note that all logical action-purpose-actor-media combinations are not necessarily possible. For example, cyberattacks cannot be undertaken through print media. The actions themselves fall into the following categories: controlling the means of communication; cyber or electronic warfare; disinformation and propaganda; positive messaging and truth-based propaganda; and defenses, counterinformation, or responses.

TABLE 3.2

Activities, Motivations, and Actors Related to Information or Operations in the Information Environment

Category	Information- or OIE-Related Activity
Controlling the means of communication	• Buying TV or movie studios, distribution networks, or TV or radio stations to control content and dissemination • Leveraging market clout to ensure positive media portrayals • Censorship, including controlling or restricting internet access
Cyber or electronic warfare	• Distributed denial of service attacks • Website vandalism or content insertion (e.g., hacking a legitimate news site to post a false story) • Seeding or distributing destructive malware; creating backdoors or other network or system vulnerabilities • Hacking user accounts and exploiting them, including to amplify messages or change attribution • Cyberbullying and other harassment of individuals, including doxxing (public exposure of private contact information or other personally identifiable information) • Hacking for espionage (or industrial espionage) • Jamming or other electronic warfare • Other unspecified offensive cyber operations
Disinformation and propaganda	• Planting, distributing, or promoting fabricated or misleading news stories or accounts • Making false accusations or charges against governments, military forces, firms, or individuals, including "exposing" misdeeds that did not occur, such as through false atrocity videos • Partial or complete forgeries, including deepfakes, doctored photos, and falsely attributed material • Spreading rumors and conspiracy theories

Table 3.2—Continued

Category	Information- or OIE-Related Activity
Disinformation and propaganda (continued)	• Promoting revisionist history or divisive or contentious historical narratives • Promoting both sides (or just the more contentious side) of a contentious issue; highlighting events (factual or otherwise) that cast a target in an unfavorable light • Amplifying or promoting certain messages, views, or narratives; disrupting, suppressing, or distracting from others • Posting execution videos or other propaganda to shock, intimidate, or punish • False defensiveness or playing the victim • Denial/*maskirovka* [deception], including flooding the information space to muddy the facts around a particular event
Positive messaging and truth-based propaganda	• Messaging themes, narratives, views, accounts, or explanations of events • Offering legitimate and valid alternatives (philosophical and actual) to the dissatisfied and disenfranchised • Disseminating videos or imagery of successful operations; touting war trophies or accomplishments • Promoting cultural information and influence, including language training, funding language schools or cultural centers, or organizing cultural or educational exchanges
Defenses, counterinformation, or responses	• Promoting media literacy, civics education, resilience, and inoculation against malign influence • Building partner capacity for journalism and local media; promoting fact-checking organizations • Conducting defensive cyber operations, including active defense, or "hacking back" to stop cyberattacks, confirm attribution, or gather intelligence about an aggressor • Reporting or enforcing terms-of-service violations • Publicizing and attributing competitor atrocities, missteps, bad deeds, or ambiguous actions • Issuing refutations, retractions, or denials

Motivations and Participants	Examples
Purposes of OIE	• "War on information": efforts to undermine credibility of all sources, pollute the IE, and promote "truth decay" • Obfuscation (in general or of something specific) or diversion • Reducing attention on a topic or event or limiting reporting and participation in public discourse by journalists, citizens, or academics with contrary views • Influence through persuasion • Influence through manipulation, coercion, deception, misdirection, intimidation, or reflexive control • Shaping public opinion or public narratives either for or against an actor or action • Discrediting, undermining, or bolstering institutions, organizations, groups, leaders, parties, companies or their views • Undermining or bolstering national will to fight, military will to fight, or military morale • Frightening, inciting, or dividing populations or intensifying or assuaging their grievances • Signaling or acting for effect

Table 3.2—Continued

Motivations and Participants	Examples
Purposes of OIE (continued)	• Encouraging individuals or organizations to engage in harassment, propaganda, or cultural promotion • Rallying one's own domestic constituency • Influencing local or national political outcomes (elections or policies), including fomenting political or other unrest • Disrupting C2, communications, or commerce • Creating strategic, operational, or tactical surprise
Actors	• Government or military personnel • Official government or military representatives/spokespersons • State-owned enterprises, semi-private firms, government contractors • Private firms or individuals (mobilized as a militia, encouraged by state actors, or undirected/uncontrolled) • Nongovernmental organizations or elements of civil society • Proxies, paid or otherwise • Bots or zombies (including astroturfing) • Human-curated false social media personas • Politicians, broadcasters, journalists, popular artists, academics, or other influencers who have been co-opted, corrupted, or coerced or have become unwitting supporters
Media	• Internet and websites, including dark web • Social media, including direct messaging and targeted campaigns; blogs, discussion boards, and dark web social networks • Print media, including magazines, newspapers, handbills, billboards, flyers, and leaflets • Broadcast media, including state-controlled news channels • Inauthentic websites, false-flag or cutout media sources • Religious, social, or cultural institutions (such as Confucius Institutes) • Film and TV studios and distribution networks • Advertising or public service announcements (in any medium), including direct advertising, social media advertising, and microtargeting • Informal networks, word of mouth

SOURCES: Analysis and synthesis of actions described in Hromadske.tv, "Peter Pomerantsev: Russia Uses Information as a Weapon," YouTube video, October 6, 2014; White House, "The Assad Regime's Use of Chemical Weapons on April 4, 2017," declassified intelligence report, Washington, D.C., April 11, 2017; "Libya, Migrants and Karma: Europe's New Migration Policy Wrecks on North African Reality," RT, July 22, 2018; Steve Abrams, "Beyond Propaganda: Soviet Active Measures in Putin's Russia," Connections, Vol. 15, No. 1, Winter 2016; Anderson and Sadjadpour, 2018; Matthew Armstrong, "Russia's War on Information," War on the Rocks, December 15, 2014; Aubrey Belford, Saska Cvetkovska, Biljana Sekulovska, and Stevan Dojčinović, "Leaked Documents Show Russian, Serbian Attempts to Meddle in Macedonia," Organized Crime and Corruption Reporting Project, June 4, 2017; Giorgio Bertolin, "Conceptualizing Russian Information Operations: Info-War and Infiltration in the Context of Hybrid Warfare," IO Sphere, Summer 2015; Dan Blumenthal, American Enterprise Institute, "China's Censorship, Propaganda, and Disinformation," statement before the Subcommittee on State Department and USAID Management, International Operations, and Bilateral International Development, Committee on Foreign Relations, U.S. Senate, Washington, D.C., March 5, 2020; Brands, 2016; Stephen Castle, "A Russian TV Insider Describes a Modern Propaganda Machine," New York Times, February 13, 2015; Mike Collier and Mary Sibierski, "NATO Allies Come to Grips with Russia's 'Hybrid Warfare,'" Agence France-Presse, March 18, 2015; Connell and Evans, 2015; Cordesman and Hwang, 2021; Jolanta Darczewska, The Devil Is in the Details: Information Warfare in the Light of Russia's Military Doctrine, Warsaw, Poland: Centre for Eastern Studies, May 2015; Christopher Davis, "Not by Force Alone: Russian Strategic Surprise in Ukraine," Modern War Institute at West Point, May 17, 2014; Joshua Davis, "Hackers Take Down the Most Wired Country in Europe,"

Table 3.2—Continued

Wired, August 21, 2007; Francisco de Borja Lasheras, Vessela Tcherneva, and Fredrik Wesslau, *Return to Instability: How Migration and Great Power Politics Threaten the Western Balkans*, Brussels, Belgium: European Council on Foreign Relations, March 2016; Dunigan et al., forthcoming; Giles, 2017; Keir Giles, *Handbook of Russian Information Warfare*, Rome, Italy: NATO Defense College, November 2016; Hoffman, 2014; Brian Michael Jenkins, *America's Great Challenge: Russia's Weapons of Mass Deception*, workshop summary report, Washington, D.C., 2019; Ieva Bērzina, Māris Cepurītis, Diana Kaljula, and Ivo Juurvee, *Russia's Footprint in the Nordic-Baltic Information Environment, Report 2016/2017*, Riga, Latvia: NATO Strategic Communications Centre of Excellence, January 2018; Jeff Kao and Mia Shuang Li, "How China Built a Twitter Propaganda Machine Then Let It Loose on Coronavirus," *ProPublica*, March 26, 2020; Jennifer Kavanagh and Michael D. Rich, *Truth Decay: An Initial Exploration of the Diminishing Role of Facts and Analysis in American Public Life*, Santa Monica, Calif.: RAND Corporation, RR-2314-RC, 2018; Andrei Kolesnikov, "Our Dark Past Is Our Bright Future: How the Kremlin Uses and Abuses History," Carnegie Moscow Center, 2020; Martin Kragh and Sebastian Åsberg, "Russia's Strategy for Influence Through Public Diplomacy and Active Measures: The Swedish Case," *Journal of Strategic Studies*, Vol. 40, No. 6, 2017; Dave Lee, "The Tactics of a Russian Troll Farm," BBC News, February 16, 2018; James Marchant, Amin Sabeti, Kyle Bowen, John Kelly, and Rebekah Heacock Jones, *#IranVotes: Political Discourse on Iranian Twitter During the 2016 Parliamentary Elections*, Cambridge, Mass.: Berkman Center for Internet and Society, Harvard University, June 2016; Mazarr, 2015; Michael J. Mazarr, Ryan Michael Bauer, Abigail Casey, Sarah Heintz, and Luke J. Matthews, *The Emerging Risk of Virtual Societal Warfare: Social Manipulation in a Changing Information Environment*, Santa Monica, Calif.: RAND Corporation, RR-2714-OSD, 2019; Metz, 2017; Morris et al., 2019; UK National Cyber Security Centre, "Russian Military 'Almost Certainly' Responsible for Destructive 2017 Cyber Attack," February 14, 2018; Olson, 2015; Christopher Paul, Colin P. Clarke, Michael Schwille, Jakub P. Hlávka, Michael A. Brown, Steven S. Davenport, Isaac R. Porche III, and Joel Harding, *Lessons from Others for Future U.S. Army Operations in and Through the Information Environment: Case Studies*, Santa Monica, Calif.: RAND Corporation, RR-1925/2-A, 2018; Perry, 2015; Pettyjohn and Wasser, 2019; Pavel Polityuk, Oleg Vukmanovic, and Stephen Jewkes, "Ukraine's Power Outage Was a Cyber Attack: Ukrenergo," Reuters, January 18, 2017; Pomerantsev, 2015; Russkiy Mir Foundation, "Russian Centers of the Russkiy Mir Foundation," webpage, undated; Schadlow, 2015; Hamza Shaban, Craig Timberg, and Elizabeth Dwoskin, "Facebook, Google and Twitter Testified on Capitol Hill. Here's What They Said," *Washington Post*, October 31, 2017; Terrell Jermaine Starr, "How Russia Weaponizes Fake News," *Jalopnik*, March 8, 2017; Robert Szwed, *Framing of the Ukraine-Russia Conflict in Online and Social Media*, Riga, Latvia: NATO Strategic Communications Centre of Excellence, May 2016; Timothy L. Thomas, *Russian Military Thought: Concepts and Elements*, McLean, Va.: MITRE Corporation, August 2019; Patrick Tucker, "Russia Pushing Coronavirus Lies as Part of Anti-NATO Influence Ops in Europe," *Defense One*, March 26, 2020; U.S. Army Special Operations Command, 2014; Daniel Victor, "Why You Shouldn't Trust 'Polls' Conducted Online," *New York Times*, September 28, 2016; Wasser et al., 2019; Wieck, 2017; Kim Willsher and Jon Henley, "Emmanuel Macron's Campaign Hacked on Eve of French Election," *The Guardian*, May 6, 2017.

Table 3.3 is the first of two tables summarizing the gray zone activities associated with the military element of national power. Because the focus is unconventional warfare, irregular warfare, and efforts to counter these kinds of activities, law enforcement and intelligence-related actions are also included. The categories are unconventional warfare, intelligence and counterintelligence, and counter–unconventional warfare and response.

TABLE 3.3

Unconventional Military Activities, Including Law Enforcement and Intelligence

Category	Unconventional Military Activities
Unconventional warfare	• Developing and sustaining ties to criminal networks or engaging in criminal activity to earn money, gain intelligence, or act as agents, including fraud, blackmail, and other financial crimes • Corrupting or infiltrating elites, government forces, and institutions or other forms of subversion • Assassinating politicians, dissidents, critics, activists, journalists, and former officials • Sabotage, especially against critical infrastructure • Providing or withdrawing support (materiel support or expressions of support) for friendly foreign elements, including clandestine support or support to militaries, paramilitaries, militias, political parties, nongovernmental organizations, separatists, or co-ethnics

Table 3.3—Continued

Category	Unconventional Military Activities
Unconventional warfare (continued)	• Infiltrating troops or materiel, including perfidious infiltration under the guise of humanitarian or medical operations • Infiltrating or employing forces without state attribution ("little green men") • Organizing a coup or otherwise overthrowing a government • Organizing or encouraging protests and demonstrations • Shadow governance or shadow provision of community services • Bullying or harassment with civilian or law-enforcement assets (coast guard, fishing fleets, border police) • Military harassment, usually unacknowledged by both sides (ships passing at unsafe distances, fighters "buzzing" ships or troops) • Offering incentives for the capture, arrest, detention, or death of adversaries
Intelligence and counterintelligence	• Collecting intelligence, surveillance, or reconnaissance • Conducting counterintelligence operations, including with capabilities and authorities to identify and expel or otherwise deal with provocateurs • Destroying or disabling competitor collection assets, including shooting down drones and satellites • Espionage, including industrial espionage • Intelligence sharing internally with other government entities or law enforcement, or externally with allies, partners, and international organizations • Building partner capacity for intelligence collection and analysis
Counter– unconventional warfare and response	• Threatening, detaining, or restricting access by journalists in targeted country • Identifying, monitoring, intimidating, or detaining dissidents • Foreign internal defense and security assistance, including providing resources to free assets for partner domestic response and training local security forces to respond appropriately to protests • Countering corruption and promoting governance and democracy, including building partner capacity for governance, rule of law, and internal security • Tracing and blocking financing for fomenting division, hiring proxies, and provocation campaigns • Offering rewards for information leading to the capture of criminals, fugitives, terrorists, or insurgents • Providing or improving community services and governance • Conducting law enforcement/security patrols, investigating possible unconventional warfare actions • Legitimate peacekeeping

SOURCES: Analysis and synthesis of actions described in "Montenegro Begins Trial of Alleged Pro-Russian Coup Plotters," Reuters, July 19, 2017; Peter Apps, "'Ambiguous Warfare' Providing NATO with New Challenge," Reuters, August 21, 2014; David Barno, "The Shadow Wars of the 21st Century," *War on the Rocks*, July 23, 2014; Brands, 2016; Connell and Evans, 2015; Cordesman and Hwang, 2021; Darczewska, 2015; C. Davis, 2014; Dunigan et al., forthcoming; Galeotti, 2015; Roy Greenslade, "Journalists Covering the Ukraine Crisis Suffer Intimidation," *The Guardian*, July 23, 2014; Elias Groll, "A Brief History of Attempted Russian Assassinations by Poison," *Foreign Policy*, March 9, 2018; Kerin Hope, "Russia Meddles in Greek Town to Push Back the West," *Financial Times*, July 13, 2018; Scott Jasper and Scott Moreland, "The Islamic State Is a Hybrid Threat: Why Does That Matter?" *Small Wars Journal*, December 2, 2014; Alexandra Jolkina and Markian Ostaptschuk, "Activists or Kremlin Agents—Who Protects Russian-Speakers in the Baltics?" *Deutsche Welle*, December 9, 2015; Kennan, 1948b; Joshua Kucera, "U.S. Intelligence: Russia Sabotaged BTC Pipeline Ahead of 2008 Georgia War," *EurasiaNet*, December 11, 2014; Mazarr, Casey, et al., 2019; Mazarr, 2015; Morris et al., 2019; Paul, Clarke, Schwille, et al., 2018; Pettyjohn and Wasser, 2019; Pomerantsev, 2015; Schadlow, 2015; Simon Shuster, "How Russian Voters Fueled the Rise of Germany's Far-Right," *Time*, September 25, 2017; Thomas, 2019; U.S. Army Special Operations Command, 2014; U.S. Army Special Operations Command, 2015; Wasser et al., 2019; Ivan Watson and Sebastian Shukla, "Russian Fighter Jets 'Buzz' US Warship in Black Sea, Photos Show," CNN, February 16, 2017.

Table 3.4 presents our enumeration of conventional military activities that are relevant to strategic competition. Although the list includes "direct military confrontation" as an activity, this is only because, in the spectrum from cooperation through competition to conflict, competition walks right up to the line of conflict. The table includes three categories: using conventional military forces for threats or signals, deterrence, or coercion and compellence; bolstering allies or one's own capabilities; and conventional military aggression.

TABLE 3.4
Conventional Military Activities

Category	Conventional Military Activities
Using conventional forces for threats/ signals, deterrence, coercion/ compellence	• Military exercises, including regular exercises, snap exercises, training missions, and exercises near borders • Prepositioning supplies/logistics • Mobilizing troops, deploying forces, or enhancing force posture, rotationally or on a permanent basis • Aggressive (or counteraggressive) movement or massing of troops • Conducting freedom-of-navigation operations • Conducting port calls • Holding military parades/shows of force/military intimidation • Establishing or enforcing anti-access/area-denial or no-go zones; imposing blockades, including mining straits or other transit routes • Investing in or acquiring deterrent or denial technology, such as hypersonic or nuclear weapons
Bolstering allies or one's own capabilities	• Conducting joint exercises with allies and partners • Building partner capacity, including military-to-military engagements and train-and-advise missions • Arms transfers and sales • Creating new military units or reorganizing existing units • Increasing military spending or undertaking modernization efforts • Militarizing society, including through compulsory service and compulsory reserve service for veterans
Conventional military aggression	• Direct military confrontation with hostile forces • Seizing terrain and de facto control of it (fait accompli) or creeping borders • Providing military cover for secession, occupying a contested area with troops, or using troops for disingenuous "peacekeeping" or "crisis regulation" • Creating and sustaining frozen conflicts as a source of persistent instability

SOURCES: Analysis and synthesis of actions described in Connell and Evans, 2015; Dunigan et al., forthcoming; Valery Gerasimov, "The Value of Science in Prediction," *Military-Industrial Kurier*, February 27, 2013; Thomas Goltz, "Letter from Eurasia: The Hidden Russian Hand," *Foreign Policy*, No. 92, Autumn 1993; David M. Herszenhorn, "Crimea Votes to Secede from Ukraine as Russian Troops Keep Watch," *New York Times*, March 16, 2014; International Crisis Group, *Moldova's Uncertain Future*, Brussels, Belgium: Europe Report No. 175, August 17, 2006; Stephanie Joyce, "Along a Shifting Border, Georgia and Russia Maintain an Uneasy Peace," National Public Radio, March 13, 2017; Laura Mallonee, "Meet the People of a Soviet Country That Doesn't Exist," *Wired*, March 7, 2016; Mazarr, 2015; Morris et al., 2019; Organization for Security and Co-operation in Europe, *Istanbul Document 1999*, Istanbul, Turkey, January 2000; Robert Orttung and Christopher Walker, "Putin's Frozen Conflicts," *Foreign Policy*, February 13, 2015; Pettyjohn and Wasser, 2019; Pierce, Douds, and Marra, 2015; Thomas, 2019; U.S. Joint Chiefs of Staff, 2018; Wasser et al., 2019; Wieck, 2017.

Table 3.5 lists the economic activities we identified. In the table, these activities are divided into two categories: leveraging economic position to influence others or impose economic costs and bolstering one's own or a partner's economic position or response to economic coercion.

TABLE 3.5
Economic Activities

Category	Economic Activities
Leveraging economic position to influence others or impose economic costs	• Gaining a controlling interest in critical economic sectors or penetrating supply chains • Providing economic, military, or civil aid or assistance, such as to establish or entrench patron-client relationships or dependencies • Economic coercion, including strategically granting or withholding aid, controlling access to markets, energy coercion (pipeline diplomacy/energy blackmail), or imposing formal or informal economic consequences • Leveraging state-owned or state-influenced enterprises to compete unfairly or impose costs on competitors (or their firms)
Bolstering one's own or a partner's economic position or response to economic coercion	• Providing economic, military, or civil aid or assistance with no implied coercion • Offering aid, compensatory economic benefits, or alternatives to countries targeted by a competitor's economic coercion • Targeting investments to catch up or get ahead in specific fields; securing natural resources • Pushing to diversify trade partners or pursue alternate or additional energy sources

SOURCES: Analysis and synthesis of actions described in "Russia's Sberbank to Get 40 Pct of Croatia's Agrokor After Debt Conversion," Reuters, June 8, 2018; "UPDATE 3—Russia Raises Gas Prices for Ukraine by 80 Percent," Reuters, April 3, 2014; Cordesman and Hwang, 2021; Darczewska, 2015; Dunigan et al., forthcoming; Freedberg, 2018; Kennan, 1948b; Mazarr, 2015; Morris et al., 2019; Pettyjohn and Wasser, 2019; Andrew Radin, Alyssa Demus, and Krystyna Marcinek, *Understanding Russian Subversion: Patterns, Threats, and Responses*, Santa Monica, Calif.: RAND Corporation, PE-331-A, 2020; Schadlow, 2015; Wasser et al., 2019.

CHAPTER FOUR

An Overview of Challenges

Our synthesis of the literature revealed several challenges posed by the activities listed in Chapter Three, along with the nature of competition and the characteristics of the contemporary competitive environment.

Many DoD Authorities Are Tied to a Peace/War Binary Rather Than a Competition Continuum

DoD continues to be constrained by an artificially sharp distinction between armed military conflict and peace.[1] This binary construct has traditionally permeated authorities, investments, forces, and organizing structures across the joint force. It has hindered the creation of forces needed to operate effectively in the context of competition, saddled operational commands with significant bureaucratic restrictions, and limited the response options available to commanders. Mark Laity, former chief of strategic communications at Supreme Headquarters Allied Powers Europe, noted in 2016 that U.S. doctrine did not permit DoD to undertake what Russia considers information confrontation activities "till the fighting basically starts."[2] This is because, traditionally, DoD's authority to conduct many of the activities discussed in the previous chapter is tied to wartime authorities and thus requires some kind of declaration of active hostilities. DoD has begun to take steps to address this challenge, seeking to end the peace-or-war dichotomy and promulgate doctrine and concepts acknowledging that competition and conflict occur on a spectrum.[3] We understand that some changes after Laity's 2016 remarks have improved this situation, but there is more to be done.

Meanwhile, U.S. adversaries and competitors are acutely aware of these constraints, operate in ways that exploit this artificial distinction, and avoid triggering a U.S. military response. For example, Russian officials operate with the notion that open conflict does not need to be declared for hostile activity in the information space to occur.[4] In this phase of

---

[1] Joint Doctrine Note 1-19, 2019, p. 1.

[2] Giles, 2016, p. 11.

[3] See, for example, U.S. Joint Chiefs of Staff, 2018.

[4] Giles, 2016, p. 10.

"information confrontation," a period of persistent struggle for information superiority over rivals, Russia's conception of what is acceptable allows it to employ a variety of hostile tactics before the onset of military conflict.[5] In effect, Russia uses all the capabilities at its disposal for information confrontation and does not perceive the state of relations between nations through the same lens as the United States.[6] Russia and China are both organized in a way that allows them to easily leverage all elements of national power in a coordinated manner even short of active conflict.

Ambiguity Creates Dilemmas

Ambiguity is one of the consensus characteristics of gray zone aggression because ambiguity is effective. It is very difficult to calculate appropriate and calibrated responses when the details of a situation are unclear. Even if a situation is fully understood, it can still be difficult to decide what to do. Creeping incrementalism creates constant dilemmas: If a competitor's gray zone activities are clearly below the threshold that would trigger an escalation to conflict, which ones warrant a response and when?[7] If a competitor is constantly taking small aggressive nibbles or "salami slices," a single aggregate response to the accumulated nibbling risks appearing disproportionate. Put another way, if an aggressor's small aggressions become the baseline and difficult to distinguish from background noise, then a U.S. response to those actions risks being viewed as aggressive rather than responsive.

Attribution Can Be Difficult

One obvious response to ambiguity is to disambiguate. That response generally has merit. However, it is easier to say than do in certain circumstances, particularly when it comes to assigning attribution. Attribution can be particularly challenging in cyberspace, with its opportunities for anonymity and the use of proxies, unwitting pawns, and private citizens acting on their own initiative. There is also a question of the burden of proof. It might be sufficient to use circumstantial evidence to make a public accusation, but pursuing a criminal case could take years of rigorous investigation and meticulous evidence collection—if it is even possible to identify the individuals responsible. A different standard entirely might apply to clandestine activities, to which the United States is freer to quietly reply in kind. Further complicating attribution are the sources and methods used to uncover the culprits. The intelligence community might be able to provide senior leaders with classified assessments,

---

[5] See Defense Intelligence Agency, *Russia Military Power: Building a Military to Support Great Power Aspirations*, Washington, D.C., DIA-11-1704-161, 2017, pp. 38–39.

[6] Giles, 2016, p. 4.

[7] Mazarr, 2015.

but publicly sharing conclusions about who is responsible for a cyberattack or other act of hostility could reveal the source or methods used to collect the evidence. Lengthy investigation or long-term monitoring of a situation might eventually reveal the parties responsible, but it can enable a fait accompli wherein the aggressor's objectives are achieved before attribution or a response can occur.

Defenders Cannot Defend Everywhere Equally Rigorously

Principles of maneuver warfare give the advantage to the offense, with the attacking force applying strength to weakness and exploiting gaps. The same principles apply to competition and give advantages to the aggressor. Revisionist powers have historically taken incremental steps toward achieving their objectives, and they can be highly opportunistic. They watch for weaknesses or moments of distraction or vulnerability, or they can simply seek out areas of the competitive space that are less of a priority for defenders. Vladimir Lenin is often credited with saying, "You probe with bayonets. If you find mush, you push. If you find steel, you withdraw."[8] This poses a daunting challenge for defenders. The United States cannot defend (or compete) everywhere with equal rigor, so aggressive competitors will certainly be able to find vulnerabilities and make progress in the gaps in U.S. attention and away from critical interests.[9]

Creeping Incrementalism and Everyday Gradualism Are Difficult to Deter

Occasional, ambiguous, and limited aggressions are similarly difficult to deter. RAND colleagues have written that

> the characteristics of everyday gray zone tactics—they are largely nonmilitary, usually gradual, and difficult to decisively attribute—lower the stakes and make it difficult for the West to credibly threaten to punish Russia, even if the actions are conclusively traced back to Moscow.[10]

Once gains have been realized, compelling a competitor to relinquish them raises the additional challenge of trying to reverse a fait accompli.

Note that creeping incrementalism is a way to effect change. Not only are such actions difficult to deter, but they inherently favor revisionist powers over those attempting to preserve the status quo.

---

[8] It is debatable whether Lenin actually spoke these words, and the quote is transliterated various ways.

[9] Connable et al., 2020.

[10] Pettyjohn and Wasser, 2019, p. ix.

Competition Takes Place Under the Nuclear Umbrella

One of the distinguishing characteristics of gray zone activities is that they intentionally fall below the threshold of war and seek to avoid escalation. However, the threat of escalation—specifically, escalation all the way to nuclear conflict—hangs over the contemporary competitive context. RAND colleagues have cautioned, "Russia's nuclear arsenal provides it with a high degree of immunity to direct military coercion. Although Russia is a much weaker state than the 20th-century Soviet Union or 21st-century China, it cannot be brushed aside or ignored."[11] The same is of course true of China and, to some extent, North Korea. Although this constraint also protects the United States and the core of the NATO alliance from direct military coercion, it acts as a significant constraint on conventional military responses to some gray zone activities.

An Episodic or Discrete Event Mindset Is Inappropriate for Enduring Competition

For revisionist powers, creeping incrementalism is all about taking little "bites" or "nibbles" of progress toward a goal without always having that progress wiped out by a response. Coercive gradualism is a long-term effort, composed of a campaign of periods of creeping advance followed by periods of quiescence and, perhaps, an opportunistic rush. The traditional DoD "force-in-readiness" or "crisis-response" perspective does not work well against such a campaign. As a report by the Defense Science Board has noted, "The Gray Zone is a challenging place for the DoD, since the U.S. tends to treat each incursion as a discrete event and then ask if that event is a threat to American strategic national interests." Instead, leaders should ask, "What is the cumulative effect of these actions and what should the U.S. do about it?"[12]

Addressing this challenge will require the U.S. government and DoD planning and response apparatus to stop viewing aggressions as separate episodes or discrete events rather than as a long-term campaign.

Gray Zone Activities Employ a Mix of Elements of Power

The final challenge that we examine in this chapter is inherent in the diversity of ways to pursue competitive ends. As noted earlier, states engaged in strategic competition use all types of national power. This poses at least two problems for the United States. First, it raises the question of who in the U.S. government is responsible for monitoring, responding to, and participating in strategic competition. Looking at individual gray zone activities, it is difficult

---

[11] Dobbins, Shatz, and Wyne, 2019, p. 8.

[12] Defense Science Board, 2016, p. 11.

but not impossible to assign responsibilities to specific government departments or agencies. However, such an approach magnifies the separate challenge of the U.S. tendency to treat events as discrete rather than as part of an incremental campaign. Further complicating matters, perspectives on a given situation can vary widely, as we found in our interviews, and that can make it difficult to agree on, plan, and coordinate a response. Interagency coordination is a common challenge in any context when it comes to developing and implementing overarching strategies, sharing information across agencies, and creating structures or organizations to facilitate collaboration.[13]

The question of who should take the lead in responding to a long-term campaign of aggression also remains. In practice, many of the executive departments of the U.S. government maintain limited expeditionary capabilities and lack the expertise to plan or manage C2 for continuous operations, with the exception of DoD. It is entirely likely that DoD will continue to be the responder of last resort rather than the responder of choice merely because it has the requisite depth of capability, especially when it comes to planning and C2.[14]

All these challenges can be exacerbated by differences in institutional cultures and lines of authority in U.S. government executive departments, where each secretary reports to the President only and not to any of the other executive departments. Coordinating across and between departments and organizations is a perennial challenge—and one that constrains U.S. effectiveness in competition.[15]

---

[13] U.S. Government Accountability Office, *National Security: Key Challenges and Solutions to Strengthen Interagency Collaboration*, Washington, D.C., GAO-10-822T, June 2010.

[14] Nathan Freier, "The Defense Identity Crisis: It's a Hybrid World," *Parameters*, Vol. 39, No. 3, Autumn 2009.

[15] Cordesman and Hwang, 2021.

CHAPTER FIVE

Possible Solutions

In the literature on competition, there is no shortage of challenges to U.S. efforts, but many of these sources also offer solutions and suggestions, which we have synthesized here.

Restructure and Reauthorize for the Competition Continuum

In an environment characterized by competition short of armed conflict, DoD's traditional focus on the conflict end of the spectrum and the limited authorities it has to operate below that threshold inhibit its ability to contribute to U.S. competition. DoD (and the authorities granted to it) must continue to shift away from the binary peace-or-war mindset and toward one that supports "enduring competition conducted through a mixture of cooperation, competition below armed conflict, and armed conflict."[1] This is what Joint Doctrine Note 1-19 terms the *competition continuum*, which consists of three parts.

The first is *armed conflict*, defined as the employment of military force in pursuit of policy objectives.[2] The second is *competition below armed conflict*, typically nonviolent actions (including diplomatic or economic activities, political subversion, and OIE) with the intent to avoid armed conflict in pursuit of policy objectives.[3] The third is *cooperation*, which can include "security cooperation activities, multinational training and exercises, information sharing, personnel exchange programs, and other peaceful military engagement activities." Of course, "Military cooperation may also occur in the form of multinational operations and activities during an armed conflict or adversarial competition."[4] The relationship between the United States and other strategic actors might span more than one of these categories.[5] For example, while the United States monitors and responds to Russian cyber operations (competition below armed conflict), the two states are engaged in active talks on nuclear nonproliferation (cooperation).

---

[1] Joint Doctrine Note 1-19, 2019, p. 2.

[2] Joint Doctrine Note 1-19, 2019, p. 2.

[3] Joint Doctrine Note 1-19, 2019, p. 2.

[4] Joint Doctrine Note 1-19, 2019, p. 3.

[5] Joint Doctrine Note 1-19, 2019, pp. 2–3.

Involve the Whole of Government

Many, many articles and studies invoke whole-of-government participation as a necessary ingredient for effective competition.[6] This follows quite sensibly from the way other competitors use capabilities from across the elements of national power; keeping up will require a similarly diverse set of capabilities.

Some studies go further and suggest an organization to lead the effort. For example, the Defense Science Board notes that "DoD has the authorities, resources, and experience to lead this effort, but it must partner with other agencies to ensure that these campaigns are targeted across all elements of national power."[7]

This is particularly important for OIE, because all organizations generate effects in and through the IE, both as part of their public outreach, public relations, or public affairs and through the actions they take. The truism that "actions speak louder than words" is a paramount consideration for coordinating OIE.

Adopt a Campaigning Mindset

A similarly large number of studies invoke the need for an integrated campaigning approach or a campaigning mindset, recognizing that competing powers string together a series of activities as part of a creeping and incremental campaign. Thus, the United States must view both the aggression and the response as part of an even larger campaign—an infinite game of sorts.[8] This is the central idea of the Joint Concept for Integrated Campaigning, in which *integrated campaigning* is defined as "Joint Force and interorganizational partner efforts to enable the achievement and maintenance of policy aims by integrating military activities and aligning non-military activities of sufficient scope, scale, simultaneity, and duration across multiple domains."[9] A campaigning approach will support coherent and sustained strategic engagement and directly meet the challenge posed by the predominantly episodic U.S. view of others' gray zone activities.

Part of moving toward a campaigning mindset might involve changing decisionmaking models. A seminal U.S. Special Operations Command white paper on the gray zone suggests adopting language from business and a SWOT (strengths, weaknesses, opportunities, and

---

[6] See, for example, Morris et al., 2019; U.S. Army Special Operations Command, 2014; Defense Science Board, 2016; and Cordesman and Hwang, 2021.

[7] Defense Science Board, 2020, p. iii.

[8] See, for example, U.S. Joint Chiefs of Staff, 2018; Cordesman and Hwang, 2021; and Defense Science Board, 2020. For more on the game analogy, see the section "Competition Can Be Conceived as a Series of Games," in Chapter Two.

[9] U.S. Joint Chiefs of Staff, 2018, p. v.

threats) planning model for better decisionmaking.[10] If the SWOTs include events over time as part of a campaign (and in support of campaign objectives), better still.

Build and Strengthen Partnerships, Lead Through Multilateral Processes

Also appearing frequently in the literature is a call for competing as part of a coalition of mutual supporters of the current rules-based order.[11] RAND colleagues have noted that

> the concept of a rules-based order remains a highly appealing concept to rally support in Europe and Asia and offers the United States an opportunity to significantly strengthen its hand in the unfolding competition by using reactions to Chinese and Russian aggressiveness as the basis for strengthened regional postures.[12]

As discussed, aggression by revisionists makes it easier to build coalitions to respond to aggressions; the United States should seize these opportunities.

Employ Transparency

The obvious solution to the challenge of ambiguity is transparency. After all, "openness remains the best defense."[13] Transparency efforts include "naming and shaming"—exposing and attributing competitors' gray zone aggressions—to disrupt competitors' campaign approaches and history of creeping gradualism or ongoing aggression. In the name of transparency, reports also recommend explicitly supporting deterrence by communicating expectations to competitors and clearly linking actions to punishments should competitors fail to meet these expectations.[14]

Be Proactive Rather Than Reactive

As noted in our discussion of challenges, several factors advantage the aggressor over the defender. One way to surmount these challenges is to seize the initiative rather than remain-

---

[10] U.S. Special Operations Command, 2015.

[11] See, for example, Morris et al., 2019, and Dobbins, Shatz, and Wyne, 2019.

[12] Morris et al., 2019, p. xv.

[13] Joseph S. Nye, Jr., "How Sharp Power Threatens Soft Power: The Right and Wrong Ways to Respond to Authoritarian Influence," *Foreign Affairs*, January 24, 2018, p. 4.

[14] Radin, Demus, and Marcinek, 2020.

ing in a reactive posture.[15] This might involve "going on the offensive" and actively pursuing U.S. objectives as part of competition.[16] Or it could mean being rapidly reactive and posturing to respond quickly to emergent provocations.[17]

Maintain a Robust Forward Presence

Also somewhat common in the literature is the value of forward presence.[18] Maintaining forward forces and capabilities provides many possible advantages, including the ability to respond rapidly and engage proactively, as well as to reassure partners and contribute to deterrence.

Increase Risk Tolerance

The intentional ambiguity associated with most gray zone activities makes it harder for leaders to respond decisively and with confidence. Although efforts to increase transparency and closely monitor competitor activities can help, the risks associated with timely and effective responses to gray zone aggression will remain. Increased risk tolerance is a possible answer. In the words of RAND colleagues, "Any strategy for responding to gray zone aggression must balance excessive risks of escalation—including military, diplomatic, and economic aspects— with the reality that, to be effective, countering gray zone aggression demands some degree of risk tolerance."[19] This might require senior leaders to accept uncertainty and risk while choosing to act anyway, empower subordinates to act under similar conditions, and delegate permissions and authorities as needed.

Allow Responses to Cross Domains or Employ Different Elements of National Power

One important point that only a few studies make is that all competitive responses need not be in kind.[20] For example, if a competitor engages in a military gray zone activity, the United States does not need to respond militarily. Instead, the response might occur in a wholly different space. Sanctions are an example of a dual economic and diplomatic mechanism that

---

[15] Morris et al., 2019.

[16] Morris et al., 2019, p. xiii.

[17] Morris et al., 2019.

[18] See Dobbins, Shatz, and Wyne, 2019; Connable et al., 2020.

[19] Morris et al., 2019, p. xiii.

[20] See, for example, Pomerantsev, 2015.

is used to punish states that undertake unlawful military incursions. Similarly, the United States does not need to meet Russian cyber aggression on a tit-for-tat basis. It could, instead, launch a diplomatic offensive calling out and attributing the aggression or imposing costs on the aggressor in some other arena. The fundamental insight is that the aggressor should not be allowed to choose the field or the bounds. However, regardless of where or how the United States responds, to be effective, responses must be communicated as being explicitly tied to the competitor's initial action so that action and response are seen as related rather than two unconnected events.

Overextend Competitors

U.S. resources are finite, but so are those of its competitors. States that use gray zone tactics in service of competition also face trade-offs regarding their competitive activities.[21] This insight creates opportunities for the United States. First, it could seek to increase the costs of competitors' gray zone aggressions. *Costs* in this case should be interpreted broadly; for example, exposure and denouncement of a set of aggressive activities could impose reputational or credibility costs similarly to how using economic leverage can make competitors spend more money or other resources to achieve their objectives.

Second, the United States might take steps to reduce the overall pool of resources (e.g., money, political capital, prestige) available to a competitor. That is, it could employ non-violent means to stress a competitor's economy or political standing and subsequently curb aggression.[22] Note that this approach aligns closely with the previous possible solution in that it crosses domains or elements of national power.

Empower Civil Society in Partner Countries

Several contributors to the literature suggest resilience promotion as an approach to reducing the effectiveness of gray zone activities. Strong civil societies and robust democratic institutions should prevent or undermine broad swaths of possible gray zone activities.[23] Promoting good governance and bolstering civil society, in terms of "social cohesion, effective law enforcement, an independent and responsible media, and legitimate, transparent and effective governance," could help allies to better resist many forms of aggressive competition.[24]

---

[21] James Dobbins, Raphael S. Cohen, Nathan Chandler, Bryan Frederick, Edward Geist, Paul DeLuca, Forrest E. Morgan, Howard J. Shatz, and Brent Williams, *Extending Russia: Competing from Advantageous Ground*, Santa Monica, Calif.: RAND Corporation, RR-3063-A, 2019.

[22] Dobbins, Cohen, et al., 2019.

[23] Pettyjohn and Wasser, 2019.

[24] Galeotti, 2015, p. 4.

CHAPTER SIX

Implications for DoD and Future Research Directions

This report summarized and synthesized findings from our interviews and our review of the existing scholarly literature regarding strategic competition, and it presented a categorized enumeration of specific gray zone activities. It also synthesized consensus views on the many challenges of competition and presented a series of possible solutions. To conclude, we review key insights and present a few additional observations.

Across DoD organizations, there is confusion about exactly what competition is supposed to be and what DoD's role in competition should be. This confusion echoes the wide range of terms in use to describe competition and the sometimes-contradictory ideas in the related scholarly and policy literature. Despite its variety, the literature clearly converges on some central ideas:

- Competition takes place on a continuum that runs from cooperation through competition and into conflict.
- Thresholds—and the defense, management, exploitation, or stretching of thresholds—are central in competition.
- Ambiguity is inherent in competition and complicates responses to competitive acts.
- Strategic competition leverages all varieties of national power (diplomatic, informational, military, and economic), not just military power.
- Strategic competition can be conceived of as an infinite game comprising a series of finite games, some of which will be zero-sum and some of which will be positive-sum.

The nature of strategic competition poses a range of challenges for a status quo competitor like the United States. The literature proposes numerous solutions; those that involve the whole of government, adopting a campaigning mindset, and maintaining transparency have the greatest relevance for DoD's efforts related to OIE in the context of competition.

Tables 3.1–3.5 in Chapter Three provided (at a certain level of abstraction) an extensive menu of what various competitors have done as part of strategic competition and what the United States and its partners might do to advance their own interests or might do to mount a response. Understanding and categorizing various actions can provide a clearer picture of what is taking place and guide near-term responses and future longer-term contingency or campaign planning.

DoD should continue refining its concepts for competition and for OIE in the context of competition. Where this conceptual work converges, DoD will need to communicate approved constructs through published guidance (e.g., doctrine, a joint concept).[1] It will also need to seek clear authorities from Congress to execute operations as part of those concepts.

Suggestions for Further Research

This study contributed important incremental progress in the problem space where OIE and competition intersect, but that problem space remains well-occupied with challenges, many of which are ripe for further inquiry.

The lists of gray zone activities in Chapter Three do not identify which elements of DoD or the interagency community are responsible for undertaking, monitoring, or responding to particular activities. Developing and refining a list of such assignments in consultation with stakeholders from across the U.S. government could serve the dual function of identifying where responsibility is clear and where it is not. It would also provide an opportunity to engage stakeholders in considering and discussing how unclear assignments might be clarified or identifying the appropriate office to take ownership of a particular activity. A strong list of competitive activities with clear organizational divisions of responsibility would be foundational for establishing clear interagency guidance for the coordination and conduct of these activities—or the coordination of responses to competitors' use of these activities.

Additional research (and perhaps direct support) could also help DoD integrate competition and OIE during competition into joint doctrine and concepts. Research that specifically supports development of a joint concept for competition could be particularly fruitful.

Finally, while DoD needs to take steps to reduce risk aversion as part of more-rigorous strategic competition, additional research on frameworks for expressing risk, especially risks associated with OIE, could contribute to that effort.

---

[1] OIE could be adequately addressed in guidance on competition more broadly, or it might require its own guidance document.

Abbreviations

C2	command and control
DoD	U.S. Department of Defense
IE	information environment
NATO	North Atlantic Treaty Organization
OIE	operations in the information environment
OSD	Office of the Secretary of Defense
SME	subject-matter expert
USEUCOM	U.S. European Command

References

Abrams, Steve, "Beyond Propaganda: Soviet Active Measures in Putin's Russia," *Connections*, Vol. 15, No. 1, Winter 2016, pp. 5–31.

Anderson, Collin, and Karim Sadjadpour, *Iran's Cyber Threat: Espionage, Sabotage, and Revenge*, Washington, D.C.: Carnegie Endowment for International Peace, 2018.

Apps, Peter, "'Ambiguous Warfare' Providing NATO with New Challenge," Reuters, August 21, 2014.

Armstrong, Matthew, "Russia's War on Information," *War on the Rocks*, December 15, 2014. As of October 14, 2021:
https://warontherocks.com/2014/12/russias-war-on-information

Barno, David, "The Shadow Wars of the 21st Century," *War on the Rocks*, July 23, 2014. As of October 14, 2021:
https://warontherocks.com/2014/07/the-shadow-wars-of-the-21st-century

Belford, Aubrey, Saska Cvetkovska, Biljana Sekulovska, and Stevan Dojčinović, "Leaked Documents Show Russian, Serbian Attempts to Meddle in Macedonia," Organized Crime and Corruption Reporting Project, June 4, 2017. As of October 14, 2021:
https://www.occrp.org/en/spooksandspin/
leaked-documents-show-russian-serbian-attempts-to-meddle-in-macedonia

Bertolin, Giorgio, "Conceptualizing Russian Information Operations: Info-War and Infiltration in the Context of Hybrid Warfare," *IO Sphere*, Summer 2015, pp. 10–11.

Bērzina, Ieva, Māris Cepurītis, Diana Kaljula, and Ivo Juurvee, *Russia's Footprint in the Nordic-Baltic Information Environment, Report 2016/2017*, Riga, Latvia: NATO Strategic Communications Centre of Excellence, January 2018.

Blechman, Barry M., and Stephen S. Kaplan, *Force Without War: U.S. Armed Forces as a Political Instrument*, Washington, D.C.: Brookings Institution, 1978.

Blumenthal, Dan, American Enterprise Institute, "China's Censorship, Propaganda, and Disinformation," statement before the Subcommittee on State Department and USAID Management, International Operations, and Bilateral International Development, Committee on Foreign Relations, U.S. Senate, Washington, D.C., March 5, 2020. As of October 14, 2021:
https://www.aei.org/wp-content/uploads/2020/03/
DBlumenthal-Testimony-on-Chinese-Censorship-1.pdf

Brands, Hal, "Paradoxes of the Gray Zone," Foreign Policy Research Institute, February 5, 2016. As of October 14, 2021:
https://www.fpri.org/article/2016/02/paradoxes-gray-zone

Castle, Stephen, "A Russian TV Insider Describes a Modern Propaganda Machine," *New York Times*, February 13, 2015.

Charap, Samuel, "The Ghost of Hybrid Warfare," *Survival*, Vol. 57, No. 6, 2015, pp. 51–58.

Collier, Mike, and Mary Sibierski, "NATO Allies Come to Grips with Russia's 'Hybrid Warfare,'" Agence France-Presse, March 18, 2015.

Connable, Ben, Jason H. Campbell, and Dan Madden, *Stretching and Exploiting Thresholds for High-Order War: How Russia, China, and Iran Are Eroding American Influence Using Time-Tested Measures Short of War*, Santa Monica, Calif.: RAND Corporation, RR-1003-A, 2016. As of October 14, 2021:
https://www.rand.org/pubs/research_reports/RR1003.html

Connable, Ben, Stephanie Young, Stephanie Pezard, Andrew Radin, Raphael S. Cohen, Katya Migacheva, and James Sladden, *Russia's Hostile Measures: Combating Russian Gray Zone Aggression Against NATO in the Contact, Blunt, and Surge Layers of Competition*, Santa Monica, Calif.: RAND Corporation, RR-2539-A, 2020. As of October 14, 2021:
https://www.rand.org/pubs/research_reports/RR2539.html

Connell, Mary Ellen, and Ryan Evans, *Russia's "Ambiguous Warfare" and Implications for the U.S. Marine Corps*, Arlington, Va.: CNA, May 2015.

Cordesman, Anthony H., and Grace Hwang, *Chronology of Possible Chinese Gray Area and Hybrid Warfare Operations*, working draft, Washington, D.C.: Center for Strategic and International Studies, September 28, 2020.

———, *The Biden Transition and U.S. Competition with China and Russia: The Crisis-Driven Need to Change U.S. Strategy*, Washington, D.C.: Center for Strategic and International Studies, January 6, 2021.

Curtis, Richard A., "Contemporary Warfare Model—A Conceptual Framework of Modern Warfare," U.S. Air Force Special Operations School, undated.

Darczewska, Jolanta, *The Devil Is in the Details: Information Warfare in the Light of Russia's Military Doctrine*, Warsaw, Poland: Centre for Eastern Studies, May 2015.

Davis, Christopher, "Not by Force Alone: Russian Strategic Surprise in Ukraine," Modern War Institute at West Point, May 17, 2014.

Davis, Joshua, "Hackers Take Down the Most Wired Country in Europe," *Wired*, August 21, 2007.

De Borja Lasheras, Francisco, Vessela Tcherneva, and Fredrik Wesslau, *Return to Instability: How Migration and Great Power Politics Threaten the Western Balkans*, Brussels, Belgium: European Council on Foreign Relations, March 2016.

Defense Intelligence Agency, *Russia Military Power: Building a Military to Support Great Power Aspirations*, Washington, D.C., DIA-11-1704-161, 2017.

Defense Science Board, *Summer Study on Capabilities for Constrained Military Operations*, Washington, D.C., December 2016.

———, *2019 DSB Summer Study on the Future of U.S. Military Superiority*, Washington, D.C., June 2020.

Dobbins, James, Raphael S. Cohen, Nathan Chandler, Bryan Frederick, Edward Geist, Paul DeLuca, Forrest E. Morgan, Howard J. Shatz, and Brent Williams, *Extending Russia: Competing from Advantageous Ground*, Santa Monica, Calif.: RAND Corporation, RR-3063-A, 2019. As of October 14, 2021:
https://www.rand.org/pubs/research_reports/RR3063.html

Dobbins, James, Howard J. Shatz, and Ali Wyne, *Russia Is a Rogue, Not a Peer; China Is a Peer, Not a Rogue: Different Challenges, Different Responses*, Santa Monica, Calif.: RAND Corporation, PE-310-A, 2019. As of October 14, 2020:
https://www.rand.org/pubs/perspectives/PE310.html

DoD—*See* U.S. Department of Defense.

Dunigan, Molly, Brodi Kotila, Kimberly Jackson, Ashley L. Rhoades, and John J. Drennan, *Competing to Win: Coordinating and Leveraging U.S. Army Contributions to Strategic Competition*, Santa Monica, Calif.: RAND Corporation, RR-A718-1, forthcoming.

Elkus, Adam, "Abandon All Hope, Ye Who Enter Here: You Cannot Save the Gray Zone Concept," *War on the Rocks*, December 30, 2015. As of October 14, 2021:
https://warontherocks.com/2015/12/
abandon-all-hope-ye-who-enter-here-you-cannot-save-the-gray-zone-concept

Freedberg, Sydney J., Jr., "US Needs New Strategy to Combat Russian, Chinese 'Political Warfare': CSBA," *Breaking Defense*, May 31, 2018.

Freier, Nathan, "The Defense Identity Crisis: It's a Hybrid World," *Parameters*, Vol. 39, No. 3, Autumn 2009, pp. 81–94.

Freier, Nate, James Hayes, Michael Hatfield, and Lisa Lamb, "Game On or Game Over: Hypercompetition and Military Advantage," *War Room*, May 22, 2018. As of October 14, 2021:
https://warroom.armywarcollege.edu/articles/
the-new-defense-normal-nine-fundamentals-of-hypercompetition

Galeotti, Mark, "Time to Think About 'Hybrid Defense,'" *War on the Rocks*, July 30, 2015. As of October 14, 2021:
https://warontherocks.com/2015/07/time-to-think-about-hybrid-defense

Gerasimov, Valery, "The Value of Science in Prediction," *Military-Industrial Kurier*, February 27, 2013.

Giles, Keir, *Handbook of Russian Information Warfare*, Rome, Italy: NATO Defense College, November 2016.

———, "Countering Russian Information Operations in the Age of Social Media," Council on Foreign Relations, November 21, 2017. As of October 14, 2021:
https://www.cfr.org/report/countering-russian-information-operations-age-social-media

Goltz, Thomas, "Letter from Eurasia: The Hidden Russian Hand," *Foreign Policy*, No. 92, Autumn 1993, pp. 92–116.

Greenslade, Roy, "Journalists Covering the Ukraine Crisis Suffer Intimidation," *The Guardian*, July 23, 2014.

Grigas, Agnia, *Beyond Crimea: The New Russian Empire*, New Haven, Conn.: Yale University Press, 2016.

Groll, Elias, "A Brief History of Attempted Russian Assassinations by Poison," *Foreign Policy*, March 9, 2018.

Herszenhorn, David M., "Crimea Votes to Secede from Ukraine as Russian Troops Keep Watch," *New York Times*, March 16, 2014.

Hoffman, Frank G., *Conflict in the 21st Century: The Rise of Hybrid Wars*, Arlington, Va.: Potomac Institute for Policy Studies, December 2007.

———, "Hybrid Warfare and Challenges," *Joint Force Quarterly*, No. 52, First Quarter 2009, pp. 34–39.

———, "On Not-So-New Warfare: Political Warfare vs Hybrid Threats," *War on the Rocks*, July 28, 2014. As of October 14, 2021:
http://warontherocks.com/2014/07/on-not-so-new-warfare-political-warfare-vs-hybrid-threats

———, "Sharpening Our Military Edge: The NDS and the Full Continuum of Conflict," *Small Wars Journal*, June 27, 2018.

Hope, Kerin, "Russia Meddles in Greek Town to Push Back the West," *Financial Times*, July 13, 2018.

Hromadske.tv, "Peter Pomerantsev: 'Russia Uses Information as a Weapon,'" YouTube video, October 6, 2014. As of October 14, 2021:
https://www.youtube.com/watch?v=0YOwOd9m9_o

International Crisis Group, *Moldova's Uncertain Future*, Brussels, Belgium, Europe Report No. 175, August 17, 2006.

Jasper, Scott, and Scott Moreland, "The Islamic State Is a Hybrid Threat: Why Does That Matter?" *Small Wars Journal*, December 2, 2014.

Jenkins, Brian Michael, *America's Great Challenge: Russia's Weapons of Mass Deception*, workshop summary report, Washington, D.C., 2019.

Joint Doctrine Note 1-19, *Competition Continuum*, Washington, D.C.: U.S. Joint Chiefs of Staff, June 3, 2019.

Joint Publication 1, *Doctrine for the Armed Forces of the United States*, Washington, D.C.: U.S. Joint Chiefs of Staff, incorporating change 1, July 12, 2017.

Joint Publication 3-13, *Information Operations*, Washington, D.C.: U.S. Joint Chiefs of Staff, incorporating change 1, November 20, 2014.

Jolkina, Alexandra, and Markian Ostaptschuk, "Activists or Kremlin Agents—Who Protects Russian-Speakers in the Baltics?" *Deutsche Welle*, December 9, 2015.

Joyce, Stephanie, "Along a Shifting Border, Georgia and Russia Maintain an Uneasy Peace," National Public Radio, March 13, 2017.

JP—*See* Joint Publication.

Judson, Jen, "The Infinite Game: How the U.S. Army Plans to Operate in Great Power Competition," *Defense News*, March 29, 2021. As of October 14, 2021:
https://www.defensenews.com/land/2021/03/29/
the-infinite-game-how-the-us-army-plans-to-operate-in-great-power-competition

Kao, Jeff, and Mia Shuang Li, "How China Built a Twitter Propaganda Machine Then Let It Loose on Coronavirus," *ProPublica*, March 26, 2020. As of October 14, 2021:
https://www.propublica.org/article/
how-china-built-a-twitter-propaganda-machine-then-let-it-loose-on-coronavirus

Karber, Phillip, and Joshua Thibeault, "Russia's New-Generation Warfare," Association of the United States Army, May 20, 2016. As of October 14, 2021:
https://www.ausa.org/articles/russia's-new-generation-warfare

Kavanagh, Jennifer, and Michael D. Rich, *Truth Decay: An Initial Exploration of the Diminishing Role of Facts and Analysis in American Public Life*, Santa Monica, Calif.: RAND Corporation, RR-2314-RC, 2018. As of October 14, 2021:
https://www.rand.org/pubs/research_reports/RR2314.html

Kennan, George, *The Inauguration of Organized Political Warfare*, declassified archival document, Washington, D.C.: U.S. Department of State Policy Planning Staff, April 30, 1948a.

———, "Policy Planning Memorandum," declassified archival document, Washington, D.C.: U.S. Department of State Policy Planning Staff, May 4, 1948b.

Kolesnikov, Andrei, "Our Dark Past Is Our Bright Future: How the Kremlin Uses and Abuses History," Carnegie Moscow Center, 2020. As of October 14, 2021:
https://carnegie.ru/commentary/81718

Kragh, Martin, and Sebastian Åsberg, "Russia's Strategy for Influence Through Public Diplomacy and Active Measures: The Swedish Case," *Journal of Strategic Studies*, Vol. 40, No. 6, 2017, pp. 773–816.

Kucera, Joshua, "U.S. Intelligence: Russia Sabotaged BTC Pipeline Ahead of 2008 Georgia War," *EurasiaNet*, December 11, 2014. As of October 14, 2021: https://eurasianet.org/us-intelligence-russia-sabotaged-btc-pipeline-ahead-of-2008-georgia-war

Lee, Dave, "The Tactics of a Russian Troll Farm," BBC News, February 16, 2018.

"Libya, Migrants and Karma: Europe's New Migration Policy Wrecks on North African Reality," RT, July 22, 2018.

Mallonee, Laura, "Meet the People of a Soviet Country That Doesn't Exist," *Wired*, March 7, 2016.

Marchant, James, Amin Sabeti, Kyle Bowen, John Kelly, and Rebekah Heacock Jones, *#IranVotes: Political Discourse on Iranian Twitter During the 2016 Parliamentary Elections*, Cambridge, Mass.: Berkman Center for Internet and Society, Harvard University, June 2016.

Marine Corps Doctrinal Publication 1-4, *Competing*, Washington, D.C.: Headquarters, U.S. Marine Corps, December 2020.

Mazarr, Michael J., *Mastering the Gray Zone: Understanding a Changing Era of Conflict*, Carlisle Barracks, Pa.: U.S. Army War College Press, December 2015.

Mazarr, Michael J., Ryan Michael Bauer, Abigail Casey, Sarah Heintz, and Luke J. Matthews, *The Emerging Risk of Virtual Societal Warfare: Social Manipulation in a Changing Information Environment*, Santa Monica, Calif.: RAND Corporation, RR-2714-OSD, 2019. As of October 14, 2021: https://www.rand.org/pubs/research_reports/RR2714.html

Mazarr, Michael J., Jonathan Blake, Abigail Casey, Tim McDonald, Stephanie Pezard, and Michael Spirtas, *Understanding the Emerging Era of International Competition: Theoretical and Historical Perspectives*, Santa Monica, Calif.: RAND Corporation, RR-2726-AF, 2018. As of October 14, 2021: https://www.rand.org/pubs/research_reports/RR2726.html

Mazarr, Michael J., Abigail Casey, Alyssa Demus, Scott W. Harold, Luke J. Matthews, Nathan Beauchamp-Mustafaga, and James Sladden, *Hostile Social Manipulation: Present Realities and Emerging Trends*, Santa Monica, Calif.: RAND Corporation, RR-2713-OSD, 2019. As of October 14, 2021: https://www.rand.org/pubs/research_reports/RR2713.html

Meakins, Joss, *Living in (Digital) Denial: Russia's Approach to Cyber Deterrence*, London: European Leadership Network, July 2018.

Metz, Steven, "How to Deter Russia from Meddling in Democracies," *World Politics Review*, May 12, 2017.

"Montenegro Begins Trial of Alleged Pro-Russian Coup Plotters," Reuters, July 19, 2017.

Morris, Lyle J., Michael J. Mazarr, Jeffrey W. Hornung, Stephanie Pezard, Anika Binnendijk, and Marta Kepe, *Gaining Competitive Advantage in the Gray Zone: Response Options for Coercive Aggression Below the Threshold of Major War*, Santa Monica, Calif.: RAND Corporation, RR-2942-OSD, 2019. As of October 14, 2021: https://www.rand.org/pubs/research_reports/RR2942.html

Nye, Joseph S., Jr., "How Sharp Power Threatens Soft Power: The Right and Wrong Ways to Respond to Authoritarian Influence," *Foreign Affairs*, January 24, 2018.

Olson, Eric, "America's Not Ready for Today's Gray Wars," *Defense One*, December 10, 2015. As of October 14, 2021:
https://www.defenseone.com/ideas/2015/12/americas-not-ready-todays-gray-wars/124381

Organization for Security and Co-operation in Europe, *Istanbul Document 1999*, Istanbul, Turkey, January 2000.

Orttung, Robert, and Christopher Walker, "Putin's Frozen Conflicts," *Foreign Policy*, February 13, 2015.

Paskal, Cleo, "Protection from China's Comprehensive National Power Requires Comprehensive National Defence," Kalinga Institute of Indo-Pacific Studies, September 2, 2020. As of October 14, 2021:
http://www.kiips.in/research/protection-from-chinas-comprehensive-national-power-requires-comprehensive-national-defence

Paul, Christopher, "Confessions of a Hybrid Warfare Skeptic: What Might Really Be Interesting but Hidden Within the Various Conceptions of Gray Zone Conflict, Ambiguous Warfare, Political Warfare, and Their Ilk," *Small Wars Journal*, March 3, 2016.

Paul, Christopher, Colin P. Clarke, Michael Schwille, Jakub P. Hlávka, Michael A. Brown, Steven S. Davenport, Isaac R. Porche III, and Joel Harding, *Lessons from Others for Future U.S. Army Operations in and Through the Information Environment: Case Studies*, Santa Monica, Calif.: RAND Corporation, RR-1925/2-A, 2018. As of October 14, 2021:
https://www.rand.org/pubs/research_reports/RR1925z2.html

Paul, Christopher, Colin P. Clarke, Bonnie L. Triezenberg, David Manheim, and Bradley Wilson, *Improving C2 and Situational Awareness for Operations in and Through the Information Environment*, Santa Monica, Calif.: RAND Corporation, RR-2489-OSD, 2018. As of October 14, 2021:
https://www.rand.org/pubs/research_reports/RR2489.html

Paul, Christopher, Yuna Huh Wong, and Elizabeth M. Bartels, *Opportunities for Including the Information Environment in U.S. Marine Corps Wargames*, Santa Monica, Calif.: RAND Corporation, RR-2997-USMC, 2020. As of October 14, 2021:
https://www.rand.org/pubs/research_reports/RR2997.html

Perry, Bret, "Non-Linear Warfare in Ukraine: The Critical Role of Information Operations and Special Operations," *Small Wars Journal*, August 14, 2015.

Pettyjohn, Stacie L., and Becca Wasser, *Competing in the Gray Zone: Russian Tactics and Western Responses*, Santa Monica, Calif.: RAND Corporation, RR-2791-A, 2019. As of October 14, 2021:
https://www.rand.org/pubs/research_reports/RR2791.html

Pierce, William G., Douglas G. Douds, and Michael A. Marra, "Countering Gray-Zone Wars: Understanding Coercive Gradualism," *Parameters*, Vol. 45, No. 3, Autumn 2015, pp. 51–61.

Polityuk, Pavel, Oleg Vukmanovic, and Stephen Jewkes, "Ukraine's Power Outage Was a Cyber Attack: Ukrenergo," Reuters, January 18, 2017.

Pomerantsev, Peter, "Brave New War: A New Form of Conflict Emerged in 2015—From the Islamic State to the South China Sea," *The Atlantic*, December 29, 2015.

Pomerleau, Mark, "Marines Look to Dominate in Information Environment," *C4ISRNET*, April 5, 2017. As of October 14, 2021:
https://www.c4isrnet.com/c2-comms/2017/04/05/marines-look-to-dominate-in-information-environment

Radin, Andrew, Alyssa Demus, and Krystyna Marcinek, *Understanding Russian Subversion: Patterns, Threats, and Responses*, Santa Monica, Calif.: RAND Corporation, PE-331-A, 2020. As of October 14, 2021:
https://www.rand.org/pubs/perspectives/PE331.html

Ronfeldt, David, and John Arquilla, *Whose Story Wins: Rise of the Noosphere, Noopolitik, and Information-Age Statecraft*, Santa Monica, Calif.: RAND Corporation, PE-A237-1, 2020. As of October 14, 2021:
https://www.rand.org/pubs/perspectives/PEA237-1.html

"Russia's Sberbank to Get 40 Pct of Croatia's Agrokor After Debt Conversion," Reuters, June 8, 2018.

Russkiy Mir Foundation, "Russian Centers of the Russkiy Mir Foundation," webpage, undated. As of October 14, 2021:
https://russkiymir.ru/en/rucenter

Schadlow, Nadia, "The Problem with Hybrid Warfare," *War on the Rocks*, April 2, 2015. As of October 14, 2021:
https://warontherocks.com/2015/04/the-problem-with-hybrid-warfare

Schelling, Thomas C., *Arms and Influence*, New Haven, Conn.: Yale University Press, 1966.

Shaban, Hamza, Craig Timberg, and Elizabeth Dwoskin, "Facebook, Google and Twitter Testified on Capitol Hill. Here's What They Said," *Washington Post*, October 31, 2017.

Shuster, Simon, "How Russian Voters Fueled the Rise of Germany's Far-Right," *Time*, September 25, 2017.

Stanley, Zell, *An Annotated Bibliography of the Open Literature on Deception*, Santa Monica, Calif.: RAND Corporation, N-2332-NA, 1985. As of October 14, 2021:
https://www.rand.org/pubs/notes/N2332.html

Starr, Terrell Jermaine, "How Russia Weaponizes Fake News," *Jalopnik*, March 8, 2017. As of October 14, 2021:
https://jalopnik.com/how-russia-weaponizes-fake-news-1793047886

Szwed, Robert, *Framing of the Ukraine-Russia Conflict in Online and Social Media*, Riga, Latvia: NATO Strategic Communications Centre of Excellence, May 2016.

Thomas, Timothy L., *Russian Military Thought: Concepts and Elements*, McLean, Va.: MITRE Corporation, August 2019.

Tiernan, Trevor, "First Class of Information Operations Airmen Completes 14F Initial Skills Training Course," Sixteenth Air Force (Air Forces Cyber), December 17, 2020.

Tucker, Patrick, "Russia Pushing Coronavirus Lies as Part of Anti-NATO Influence Ops in Europe," *Defense One*, March 26, 2020. As of October 14, 2021:
https://www.defenseone.com/technology/2020/03/russia-pushing-coronavirus-lies-part-anti-nato-influence-ops-europe/164140

UK National Cyber Security Centre, "Russian Military 'Almost Certainly' Responsible for Destructive 2017 Cyber Attack," February 14, 2018.

"UPDATE 3—Russia Raises Gas Prices for Ukraine by 80 Percent," Reuters, April 3, 2014.

U.S. Army Special Operations Command, *Counter-Unconventional Warfare*, white paper, Fort Bragg, N.C., September 26, 2014.

———, *SOF Support to Political Warfare*, white paper, Fort Bragg, N.C., March 10, 2015.

U.S. Army Training and Doctrine Command, *Multi-Domain Battle: Evolution of Combined Arms for the 21st Century 2025–2040*, version 1.0, Fort Eustis, Va., December 2017.

U.S. Department of Defense, *Joint Concept for Operating in the Information Environment (JCOIE)*, Washington, D.C., July 25, 2018.

———, *Summary of the Irregular Warfare Annex to the National Defense Strategy*, Washington, D.C., 2020.

U.S. Government Accountability Office, *National Security: Key Challenges and Solutions to Strengthen Interagency Collaboration*, Washington, D.C., GAO-10-822T, June 2010.

U.S. Joint Chiefs of Staff, *Joint Concept for Integrated Campaigning*, Washington, D.C., March 16, 2018.

U.S. Special Operations Command, *The Gray Zone*, white paper, Washington, D.C., September 9, 2015.

Victor, Daniel, "Why You Shouldn't Trust 'Polls' Conducted Online," *New York Times*, September 28, 2016.

Von der Burchard, Hans, "EU Takes Billion-Euro Battle to Russia," *Politico*, January 5, 2018. As of October 14, 2021:
https://www.politico.eu/article/russia-sanctions-europe-trade-eu-takes-billion-euro-battle

Wasser, Becca, Jenny Oberholtzer, Stacie L. Pettyjohn, and William Mackenzie, *Gaming Gray Zone Tactics: Design Considerations for a Structured Strategic Game*, Santa Monica, Calif.: RAND Corporation, RR-2915-A, 2019. As of October 14, 2021:
https://www.rand.org/pubs/research_reports/RR2915.html

Watson, Ivan, and Sebastian Shukla, "Russian Fighter Jets 'Buzz' US Warship in Black Sea, Photos Show," CNN, February 16, 2017.

White House, "The Assad Regime's Use of Chemical Weapons on April 4, 2017," declassified intelligence report, Washington, D.C., April 11, 2017. As of October 14, 2021:
https://assets.documentcloud.org/documents/3553049/Syria-Chemical-Weapons-Report-White-House.pdf

Wieck, Brian D., "Information Operations Countermeasures to Anti-Access/Area Denial," *Strategy Bridge*, May 11, 2017. As of October 14, 2021:
https://thestrategybridge.org/the-bridge/2017/5/11/information-operations-countermeasures-to-anti-accessarea-denial

Willsher, Kim, and Jon Henley, "Emmanuel Macron's Campaign Hacked on Eve of French Election," *The Guardian*, May 6, 2017.